A Woman's Worth

Elaine Stedman

Word Books, Publisher
Waco, Texas

First Printing—March 1975
Second Printing—February 1976
Third Printing—July 1976
First Paperback Printing—October 1976

A WOMAN'S WORTH

Printed in the United States of America.

IBSN 0–87680–838–0
Library of Congress card catalog number: 74–27477

To my family and friends,
who have endured my own search
for identity,
and to the Lord Jesus Christ
in whom I have found it.

Contents

Preface

The compulsion to write this book is born out of my own experience in the business world, as wife and mother, as friend and counselor. I found a growing tension between maintaining the integrity and validity of my own personhood and wanting to relate to others in ways that did not do violence to them as whole and legitimate persons. I found that most of the help directed to women by the Christian community was addressed to symptoms, ignoring the basic issues of identity and equality and misappropriating such biblical terms as "submission" and "authority."

The church has long been remiss in giving honest and in-depth consideration to our sexuality. To fill this vacuum, many reactionary views are now being aired, and we are in danger of becoming polarized rather than balanced. The Christian point of view compromises with neither the world nor the flesh, and this is the position I desire to maintain.

I find that many women of my own generation have long since resigned themselves to the status quo, either out of despair or apathy. My own temperament, aided and abetted by the thinking, hurting people in my life, has prodded me into a relentless pursuit of biblical answers to these problems of personhood. I am thoroughly convinced that the Word of God is the supreme textbook for humanity, and that the church has far from exhausted the applications of its truth.

Women are too often addressed as nonthinking people, and much of today's appeal is to emotions rather than reason. Perhaps I have over-compensated for what I believe to be a need to engage our minds for the control of our emotions. My own womanhood has been affirmed, has indeed become an exciting adventure, in direct proportion to my love relationship with God through the Lord Jesus Christ. To know him is to love him!

I am deeply grateful to my husband, who has faithfully pastored me for twenty-five years, to Joanie, Mike, and Susan who have labored with me over this manuscript, and to multitudes of friends who have encouraged and taught me in a variety of ways. I am painfully aware of the small contribution these pages make to the vastness of this subject. I can only hope it will serve as a catalyst to encourage deep and meaningful biblical investigation and application.

—ELAINE STEDMAN

1. *Identity Crisis*

The American woman is in crisis. She is barraged with propaganda designed to incite restlessness, if not revolution. She is tantalized with palliatives ranging from pinless diapers to the presidency. The heady rhetoric of today's angry women has been exploited and expanded by the media, by uneasy but responsible men, as well as by some who seize upon this public agony for political expediency. But American women are not statistics. We are living human beings, and any corrective to our collective and/or individual distress must first be addressed to our humanity.

Women's Liberation has been a catalyst for consideration of woman's plight in every strata of society, and once again we are confronted with some aged issues in new garments. Hostile fingers are pointing to the church, and indeed to the Judeo-Christian tradition, as the instigators of male–female disruption.

Unfortunately, many of these claims can be substantiated, and will not be put off by simplistic disclaimers. By their very criticism, feminists give inadvertent testimony to the degree in which society is shaped by the church. When society is filled with angry, hurting people, the church, to whom her Lord gave the commission to be salt and light in the world, the revelation of truth and life, must take her rightful share of responsibility.

For this reason, it is imperative that those who comprise the Body of Christ give serious, painstaking (and where necessary, painful) attention to this compelling cry. We may not, we must not, take shelter in complacency and through indifference substantiate the claims of our accusers. This is not an inconsequential skirmish; it is a call to wrestle with issues affecting the basic moral structure of society.

To whom shall we go for our directive? Who can define our human identity and its function? Human opinion is at best simply arbitrary, clouded by the dust of our humanity. We are simply physicians attempting to heal ourselves, sexual beings striving to define our sexuality. We form a jury to try ourselves. A detached observer is required; there is a beam in every human eye. C. S. Lewis warns of the dangers of "chronological snobbery"; that is, the tendency to accept whatever theory is currently in vogue as necessarily valid.

The issue of identity and role, both male and female, is as ancient as Adam and Eve. Both our human identity and our function were established by creative fiat, contested and distorted by the initial rebellion of the first pair and by succeeding cultural adaptations. The creative intent has been defied, misinterpreted and distorted through human ignorance and rebellion. The result is that social inequities of every kind have been given equal time by both sexes. This is the human dilemma, private rebellion become public, the corporate revelation of the individual human heart.

In Ibsen's *A Doll's House*, written in 1879, Helmer says, "Before everything else you're a wife and a mother." Nora replies, "I don't believe that any longer. I believe that before everything else I am a human being just as much as you are. At any rate I shall try to become one." Then, leaving behind a baffled, confused, and perhaps chastened man, Nora pursues her search for identity. How readily we who are women identify with her frustration, but the drama ends as the question is posed, and we are left without answers, without definitions, because in a self-centered context there are none. It is therefore with both compassion and misgivings that we anticipate the futility of her pursuit.

For generations women have been demanding a positive answer to the question presented by Dorothy Sayers in her 1938 lecture, "Are Women Human?" Both women and men have grappled with the struggle of women to be acknowledged as completely human as men. Sigmund Freud wrote approximately twenty-six volumes trying to identify the problems of humanity. There are helpful analyses in his works, yet no identity emerges from all this effort. Many images have been projected of the female: earth mother, temptress, waif, matriarchal aggressor. Women have been characterized in extremes from bane to blessing, scourge to savior. But now that Sue, Gloria, Betty, and Germaine have become, shall we say, "household names," now that we have learned to express our outrage and define our hang-ups, are we any nearer to security and identity?

In a *Life* magazine article entitled "Women Are Learning to Express Outrage," a writer who attended numerous meetings of Women's Liberation describes her reactions: "These experiences unnerved me, despite reminders that I should not take it personally, and an understanding of what lay behind the fear and hostility. The negative reactions toward me expressed a great deal of what Women's Lib is about: women's long-suppressed anger at being used, women's sense of vulnerability and defenselessness, women's suspicion and mistrust of other women, women's insecurity, lack of confidence in their judgment, the secret fear, as one girl put it, that maybe we *are* inferior."

The greatest rigor in any society facing man and woman is uncertainty, the lack of constants and absolutes. Technology has made a significant contribution to today's relativistic madness, but the misuse of technology is a symptom, not the cause. If man is the creation of God, then we slip our moorings if we, the creatures, declare our independence of our Creator. He is our constant, our absolute. In him is truth and life, and apart from him there is neither truth nor life.

We have two alternatives in assessing our identity.

There really are but two, and they are totally different. Each provides promises, and each results in its own distinct life-style. Each requires commitment, and each precludes the other. We may attempt neutrality, but that is only an illusion. Life confronts us with the necessity of choosing. We may try to compromise, but that will result in hopeless ambivalence and fragmentation.

It is not a choice between verities. God is Truth, and apart from him there is no truth. Truth by its very nature is absolute and therefore uncompromising. To choose a God-centered identity is to opt for truth, the unfolding of reality. A self-centered identity is spurious and pseudo, counterfeit truth, camouflaged reality. It denies the truth about who we are, and alienates us from God, our Creator, by denying him his rightful prerogatives.

The fragmentation of today indicates that we were never intended to have a self-centered identity. God made us for himself, and only in relationship with him can we know who we are. He has not left us without a revelation of our identity. It is delineated in the manual (femanual, if you prefer) issued by our Maker. That manual is his Word. It is both the duty and privilege of the church to speak to societal needs from the authority and revelation of God's Word.

Prerequisite to clear understanding of his revelation is a readiness to set aside our cultural preconditioning, to be non-defensive and transparent, willing to personally respond to its incisiveness, to accept God's criteria for good rather than our own. Resistance to truth will give a negative connotation to what God is saying. In no way does God intend to strike at us with his Word. He created us with loving purpose. He offers us his unconditional acceptance; we need only receive it. We dare not presume to speak for God in the world with unacknowledged, unconfessed hostility and bitterness toward him and humanity. The church must defend neither hostile feminists nor pious pretenders cloaked in misapplied and/or misunderstood Bible phrases.

Who is equal to the task? Let none claim human infallibility! Only let us with appropriate humility and confidence that God is both Truth and Love approach his Word with positive expectancy and the awareness of our finiteness.

2. *Whose Image?*

It all began in the beginning, where God already was. The first thing revealed about God is that he is the Creator, and that he created through the process of his Word. God said . . . and it was so! God's Word is creative, powerful, sovereign. The universe exists and is upheld by the "word of his power." Our existence results from his Word. We have been trying to reverse that procedure since the beginning—to create God by *our* word, to make him in *our* image. But, as the C. S. Lewis Narnia adventures frequently remind us, God is not a tame lion. He is not, in fact, tameable. And that is precisely why he remains God, unchallenged and unchallengeable.

In the beginning was God, the Creator, Father-Mother, Sovereign. God who preexisted and transcends his creation. His Word, which is truth, dispels the darkness, and the light of truth is our very life. "Know that

the Lord is God! It is he that made us, and we are his."
(Or, "It is he that made us and not we ourselves.") "We
are his people and the sheep of his pasture."

Our whole case for identity hangs on the fact of God
as Creator, and the reason he created. Behind his creative acts are the foundations for identity. This is true
of us collectively, as groups, and as individuals. Our
concept of God governs our sense of identity and self-
worth and our identification with every other person.
The crux of our humanity is, "You shall love the
Lord your God with all your heart, with all your soul,
with all your strength and with all your mind." Our
Lord was quoting the Old Testament commandment
in which the Hebrew word for love contains a sexual
connotation. A love relationship with God is necessary
to the complete fulfillment of our humanity. The sexual connotation not only points to this truth, but also
reveals the complete and intimate relationship of a
believer with the Lord God. God is concerned with
our entire being. He created and defined every function of our humanity.

It is vital for each individual to establish this personal
relationship with God, the Creator and Redeemer, so
that it becomes the primary thrust of our lives. We
enter and we exit life alone. The personal intimacy of
our relationship with God cannot be mediated or in-
terpolated by any other person. We must learn to
confront life as his creatures, and in terms of his expectations, in order to understand life's demands.

This basic commitment to God's authority and activity in our lives will require an habitual dying to false

and secondary relationships. We must allow him pre-eminence and our relationship with him must not be violated. This is essential to our sense of identity. It is the manna of life, the constancy from which we receive our perspective, our purpose and our power. It is the only thing which will save us from entanglement in confused and naïve relationship. It is the only perspective that will save us from ourselves.

Having constrained us to the love of God, Jesus then sums up the remainder of the Ten Commandments with ". . . and love your neighbor as yourself." The cycle begins with God. Our love relationship with him teaches us to love ourselves from his perspective, as his creatures. This gives us the freedom to love ourselves and others unselfishly, and this is the *only* genuine love. Knowing that we are loved by God, and that he loves us unconditionally, we receive our true sense of worth. This frees us from the futility of trying to become something that pleases God or others, and the accompanying duplicity and pretense of trying to be something we are not and cannot be. Before God we need no masks. We can be what we are and rest in his acceptance, realizing that God sees us restored to his image by the redemptive work of the Lord Jesus Christ. This is the only source of security and identity which is invulnerable.

So the story of creation begins, and the unvarying pattern is, first the material structure, then the forms of life; first the man-of-dust, then the man-of-life; first the rib, then the mother of all living. First Adam, and then Eve. Or as Paul puts it in 1 Corinthians 15:46,

"But it is not the spiritual which is first but the physical, and then the spiritual."

> Then God said, "Let us make man in our image, after our likeness, and let them have dominion over the fish of the sea, and over the birds of the air, and over the cattle, and over all the earth and over every creeping thing that creeps upon the earth." So God created man in his own image, in the image of God he created him, male and female he created them (Genesis 1:26, 27).

From this concise and uncluttered summary of human creation we learn about the equality, the duality and mutuality of our identity as human beings. We learn of our co-dominion over the earth, and recognize that this is a delegated authority. Since we are made in the image of God, the purpose for our humanity is evident: we are the means by which God is to share himself with his creation. This puts our humanity in perspective. God is not our instrument; we are his. We exist in order to manifest the character of God to his created universe. The "God-shaped vacuum" in each of us is meant to contain the very essence of life, God himself, by whom we live and move and have our being.

We are creatures with intrinsic value quite apart from what we do. This is true because we are made in God's image, and this we know to be true of him. God rested the seventh day after his creative act not from fatigue, but to show us that in his essence he is apart from, more than, his creation—more than his works: that his identity is apart from his function. This fact, also seen in humanity, is the key to optimum existence.

It is not our role which gives us value, but who we are, in terms of our relationship with God and his creative purpose. God is concerned with who we are, with our relationship with him. Our role, or function, must proceed from this identity. We have value because he made us; we receive our worth from him, from who God is. Our sense of failure, guilt, frustration, and lack of identity come from trying to live apart from his character, from his indwelling life. In separating ourselves from his character, we are denying our creative purpose. The consummate privilege of our humanity is our fellowship with God himself. We cannot love and enjoy his creation until we have learned the transcendent joy of loving and knowing the Creator.

From this uncomplicated account in Genesis of our creation, we also learn that in order to reveal the image of God we were created male and female. This was not an arbitrary caprice on God's part, but necessary to produce a balanced revelation of his character. God is Truth, and truth is both objective and subjective, a two-sided coin, concrete and abstract. God expresses himself as Father-Mother. The totality of revelation indicates that fatherhood is essentially dominant in terms of authority; motherhood is essentially submissive in terms of receptivity and responsiveness. This is analogous to the physical relationship in which the sperm is introduced by the male, and the female "interprets" it into the fetus. All elements of God's character are in perfect balance, including masculinity and femininity. The male–female complement in humanity is an expression of this aspect of God's character. Our essential identity is in our mutual humanity; we are all creatures of God, created in his image for the express purpose of sharing his life with his creation. Our sexuality is the mode by which we express his life. This constitutes our role, or (to use a word that avoids the connotation of unreal performance) our function.

The relationship between identity and role, or function, may be compared with the relationship between faith and works. There is no discrepancy between the two, but works are the result of faith, not vice versa. Works are the mode by which faith is expressed. The validity of faith is tested by works. Faith is the foundation; works the super-structure.

What faith is to works, identity is to role. Our femaleness gives us a social function, subsidiary to and dependent upon our human identity. We are essentially spiritual beings, our bodies being simply the visible evidence of that being. In God's economy, the physical, tangible elements are the parable of the essential spiritual realities. God has made the material things to picture spiritual verities. Thus, "The heavens declare the glory of God and the firmament shows his handiwork." And we, his people, demonstrate the glory of his character as we yield ourselves as those "who have been brought from death to life, and (our) members to God as instruments of righteousness."

The purpose for our human existence has, appropriately, been assigned by creative fiat. God has chosen women, as well as men, to be the bearers of *his* image, vessels in whom *his* own life is resident, life that transcends death and brings grandeur to every dimension of our humanity, as we live for the praise of our Maker. This is the factor that determines whether we will use or abuse our sexuality.

3. *So What is Human?*

Let us now return to Ibsen's Nora, and her poignant, aching quest. What identity will Nora find in a hostile and decadent society? Having declined her role as wife and mother, will she now find security and identity in a new function? If Nora is not a human being, what sociological or philosophical ingredient will perform the desired transformation to "humanness"? If Nora is not a human being, what is she? What is a human being; does one *become* human?

Out there, she will hear such statements as, "We're not afraid to give up what's feminine to be free." And again, "Let women who wish to, and who are gratified by doing so, stay home or take subordinate jobs . . . but get this straight, this choice has nothing to do with femininity." She will also hear the theme echoed again and again that a "totally new life-style for both men and women, where submission and domination do not exist, is essential for the full realization of women's equality."

She will hear demands for a complete social revolution in America, a restructuring of the nation's family, religious, educational, political, professional, and economic frameworks. They will say, "The traditional roles which describe man as the provider, protector, leader, and woman as the mother, nest-builder and follower, result from ancient myths and misconceptions. These must be replaced by a sexless society."

From the other side of the fence, the "Pussycats" will tell her, "You are simply female. Learn how it works. The individual parts add up to the purring efficiency of the whole. Think of yourself as a switchboard with all sorts of lovely buttons and plug-ins for lighting up and making connections. The idea is to keep the lines busy but not crossed up." It is truly amazing how humanity is nothing but disruptive outside of Christ. Feminists and "Pussycats" represent two reactionary extremes. Neither is correct and both plunder rather than heal our humanity. It is a sad commentary on humanity's lostness.

Will Nora turn to religionists for her answers? There, too, she will find ambiguity and confusion of role and identity. England's Emmaline Pankhurst, relying heavily on religion, bolstered her followers with "Trust in God; She will provide." On the other hand, a Texas preacher asserts from his pulpit, uncontested by his congregation, "Flakey, that stands for female!" And an avowedly Christian psychologist teaches seminars on "Masculinity Deified," urging women and children to become puppets to the husband and father. They are to think only his thoughts, cater to his every whim, and thus grossly distort the biblical concept of submission and weaken honest manhood.

Then there are more subtle errors, intentional or innocent, which reflect a bias in the interpretation of Scriptures. Referring to 1 Corinthians 11:3–16, and specifically to verse 7, "For a man ought not to cover his head, since he is the image and glory of God; but woman is the glory of man," one man concludes: "In this passage, we are dealing with divinely established principles by which the man is the head of the woman and the woman *bears the image of the man.*" Paul hereby is interpreted as endorsing the dangerously false premise that woman was made in the image of man rather than in the image of God. Such interpretation, however, contradicts the clear statement of equality in Galatians 3:28 and the clear teaching of the Genesis account of creation. This misinterpretation occurs despite the explicit wording of Paul's statement, "woman is the glory (*not* image) of man." While this kind of exegesis may be innocent or careless, it is no less devastating. It is unfortunate that men who are qualified and able ministers should thus earn for themselves epithets such as "misogynistic" and "chauvinist." But the greater tragedy is that they unjustly project that onus to Paul who writes under the inspiration of the Holy Spirit.

The Scriptures never renege on the creative and spiritual equality of woman with man, and in these consistent declarations the woman's identity is clearly and securely established. It is in this uncompromising strength of identity that her personhood stands unchallenged and unthreatened. From the Word of God we learn that we are human beings, both man and woman, because God made us so. The purpose then of our mutual humanity is to mirror God's image, which means that we are to express his character. The sexual mode through which we give expression to God's character is our function, our role.

In the case of human creativity, the function of the "created" object is left to the discretion and prerogative of the "creator." In commerce and industry, a careful system of patents and copyrights has been devised to vouchsafe this exclusive privilege. Is not this human system of law and order a reflection of the prevailing right-of-ownership between God and his creatures? If we allow for God at all, we must recognize the intelligence and integrity of his order for the function of our humanity.

It seems altogether evident and reassuring that our God-assigned function is intended to contribute to the fulfillment and the wholeness of our humanity. The function is therefore an affirmation of our identity. Fragmented, frustrated human beings, male or female, are distortions of God's image, a violation of his creative purpose. It would seem, then, that a distorted sense of identity, either as inferiority or superiority, must be evidence of a departure from God's intention and directive.

The Genesis account of creation teaches us that the human being is more than beast, less than God.

Both man and woman are given dominion over the lesser creatures, under divine authority. We are to worship God and rule nature. Within these boundaries we are free, unthreatened, and fulfilled. Any alteration of this order inhibits and denies our humanity.

> Then the Lord God formed man of dust from the ground, and breathed into his nostrils the breath of life; and man became a living being (Genesis 2:7).

The qualifying characteristic of our humanity is that we are infused with the very life of God. This is the means by which we are intended to reflect his character, to reproduce his kind of life. This also tells us that our humanity is dependent upon God for fulfillment. Without him we are dust, lacking both significance and authority. In the worship of him, in communion with his perfection and wholeness, we find healing and authentication. It is not because he needs us, but because we need him, that God commands our worship. And our worship is a response to the God who in love shares with us his own life. This is both the basic and ultimate relationship of our lives, from which all other relationships derive their relevance.

I believe a personal relationship with God is the only authentic source of human identity, and therefore a qualitative difference between the Christian and non-Christian philosophy of life. In other words, it is not only the strongest case for identity, but, by the same token, a case for Christianity.

4. *Creative Sexuality*

Men and women are different, and we have bodies to prove it! No amount of ingenuity can conclusively rearrange the biological evidence for our physiological differences. We are biologically equipped for different and distinctive roles. This is not only true of us physically, but also emotionally and spiritually. Thus, we have certain norms, or what Margaret Mead terms "cultural universals," in society resulting from what is fundamentally true to human nature. While exceptions do exist, almost invariably the mother in our society is the principal caretaker of the child and the male is the breadwinner.

It is not my purpose to amass supportive evidence to prove or disprove cultural adaptation. However, according to *Time* magazine, March 20, 1972, "Recent research hints there may even be sex differences in the brain, which may be 'masculinized' by 'testosterone' before birth." Research indicates boy and girl babies follow a pattern of objective-subjective differences in their reactions to geometric figures vs. photographs of faces, the boys responding to objective stimuli, the girls to subjective. Study after study point to major differences between the sexes in aggression vs. spatial ability.

Personality differences are detectable at remarkably early ages, and tests have substantiated similar differences in monkeys and baboons. In the same issue of *Time* magazine, the conclusion is that these observable differences "force us to consider the possibility that some of the psychological differences between men and women may not be the product of experience alone but of subtle biological differences."

However we may wish to deny it, the issue of our sexuality is also an emotional one, which in itself substantiates that we are psycho–sexual beings. Secular investigation, however, intent on objectivity, tends to serve the purpose of the investigator, with data manipulated toward a biased end.

The Book of Genesis is one of the earliest records of sexuality. It is likely therefore to be culturally unbiased, primitive, and radical (dictionary defines radical as "of or from the root; fundamental; basic"). For the Christian, to whom God is both Truth and Love, it is a true and loving definition of who we are. God does not waste his design, as his orderly and intricate creation affirms. He did not give to the masterpiece of his creation a male–female design without some purpose, and we may be sure that this purpose is in harmony with the whole of his creative design.

In the world of nature there are countless expressions of a principle which might well be labeled "masculinity–femininity." The existence of a creation presupposes a Creator, to whom the creation would be subject. This relationship of dominance and subjection characterizes the "masculinity–feminity" principle. To illustrate, consider the response of the tide to the force of gravity; the response and dependency of all green plants to the energy of light; the moon's reflection of the glory of the sun; and the nucleus around which the electron revolves.

Our language reflects this principle in many ways. For example, we speak of the sun as masculine, whose energy in the form of light produces vegetation in "mother earth."

According to this principle, God the Creator can be thought of as masculine in relation to his creation and his creation as feminine.

The Genesis text, however, tells us that mankind was created in the image of God. It is this unique image which distinguishes us from the animal world. We share with our Creator self-consciousness, the capacity for rational thinking, and the ability to moralize and be creative. This equips us for making moral choices, and authorizes us to have dominion over all the earth. Our dominion, however, is according and subject to the sovereign authority of the Creator-God.

The essential element in maleness is the concept of

masculinity: the sovereign, loving authority of God as he relates to his people. The essential element in femaleness is the concept of femininity: the willing, reverential responsive subjection of his people to that authority. Each is equal in value. Both are necessary to complete the portrait.

> Then God said, "Let us make man in our image, after our likeness; and let *them* have dominion over the fish of the sea, and over the birds of the air, and over the cattle, and over all the earth, and over every creeping thing that creeps upon the earth" (Genesis 1:26).

This delegated authority and spiritual equality was granted to man and woman by God. The freedom to choose was a necessary corollary to that authority, involving both privilege and responsibility. Thus far, humanity's relationship to God might be defined as totally feminine, and in relation to the earth and its inhabitants, masculine.

Why, then, did God define our humanity as male–female? It would appear that this is a miniature portrayal, a microcosm, of the larger principle of masculinity–femininity. Thus, male dominance demonstrates the principle of God as sovereign over his creation, while female responsive subjection illustrates the appropriate attitude toward that authority.

The freedom to choose, making her autonomous under God, is the shadow of masculinity in the woman. The shadow of femininity is, in the man, his subjection to God's authority. For both, the male–female relationship is transcended in the spiritual realm, as the Apostle Paul tells us in Galatians 3:28: "There is neither Jew nor Greek, there is neither slave nor free, there is neither male nor female; for you are all one in Christ Jesus."

Our standing with God in Christ Jesus is not reckoned on our function. Jew, Greek, slave and free, male and female, are maintained in human relationships as *roles*, but the *identity* of each is equal before God, who sees them in Christ, without relevance to function.

Thus, we may view ourselves as intricately woven into the universal fabric of masculinity–femininity—the Creator-God's vast, inscrutable master plan in which he invests the incomparable beauty of his own character in the universe. There is an exhilarating excitement in being caught up in the magnitude of the Creator's plan. We must cry out with the Apostle Paul:

> O the depth of the riches and wisdom and knowledge of God! How unsearchable are his judgments and how inscrutable his ways! For who has known the mind of the Lord, or who has been his counselor? Or who has given a gift to him that he might be repaid?
> For from him and through him and to him are all things. To him be glory forever. Amen (Romans 11:33–36).

It is a liberating experience to see oneself from this perspective, to be relieved of the confining minutia of self-centered demands. Such a perspective removes the vexing frustration of trying to out-wit, out-maneuver, and second-guess our circumstances and relationships.

Our sexuality can be a cesspool of hostility, anxiety, destructive tension, guilt, and frustration—a tyranny which robs us of the glory of our humanity. But God meant it for good! To us, as sexual beings, God has entrusted the incredible privilege and responsibility of telling his story, painting his portrait, describing his character, for the entire universe to see. The truth about God, and ourselves, sets us free. The truth is that he is the initiator and we are the responders. He is the initiator of life, of love, of truth: "We love, because he first loved us" (1 John 4:19). Jesus said of himself: "I am the way, and the truth and the life" (John 14:6). In his nature, in his life, and in his word, truth and life eternally exist. In choosing to respond to Jesus Christ, we acknowledge him as the initiator of life, truth, and love, and these verities can only be defined in terms of who he is.

He is the Giver and we are the receivers. He is the Shepherd and we are the sheep. He is the Redeemer and we the redeemed. He is the Lover and we are the loved. The purpose of our sexuality is to tell the story of God's romance with his people. Man and woman are the climax of God's design in which he is telling over and over the ways in which he relates with loving authority to his creation.

5. *Creative Equality*

"Let *them* have dominion . . . he created *them* . . . God blessed *them* . . . and God said to *them*."

Chapter one of the handbook for humanity written by the Spirit of God defines our identity. God could have populated the earth at once with a sea of humanity, with the infinite variety of snow-flakes, all sizes, colors, and shapes. He gave us instead a common ancestry: one man, one woman, of whom we have no physical description. The words "in our image, after our likeness," indicate the spiritual nature of humanity and our implicit relationship with the Creator-God. Godlikeness was his design for us, the purpose of which would be the revelation of himself.

Embodied in humanity was the life of the Creator, by means of which we were to reign in male–female complement, under God, over all of his creation. We were not to preempt God's authority, but to express it, and to do so in terms of his character. This is the first chapter in God's love story. He shares his life and his heart with his people. He creates them, blesses them, fellowships with them, and in this context he gives them a creative function suitable to their humanity. They are given the dignity of reigning over the earth as God's servants!

At no time is there any disparity between persons, as God assigns the male–female identity. The issue is not their function, but who they are as God's persons.

It seems to me the church has been remiss in her teaching and practice of the meaning and equality of persons. It appears we have misunderstood and misconstrued the Scriptures, reading into them our own racial, sexual, and cultural prejudices with resulting inequities in all of our relationships and an improper view of ourselves. God is not the author of inequality between persons. Properly related to him, all of God's creation is in harmony and balance. Inequality between persons reflects a warped understanding of God, ourselves, and others—a misunderstanding of our identity.

A woman who sees herself from God's perspective has a secure sense of identity, and the recognition of her equality with every other person. It could be summarized in this way.

I am God's woman. He made me. I accept my unique design without resentment, knowing that God's intention toward me is loving and redemptive.

A multitude of complicated hereditary and cultural factors have combined to make me what I am, but in the end nothing and no one can thwart God's redemptive plan for me. He chose me before the foundations of the earth, destined me to be conformed to his image, and has provided me with every spiritual resource I need to be a fulfilled person and to relate to others with security and joy.

He accepts me unconditionally, not on my own merit, but because he himself settled my sin issue, and I may rest in his forgiveness. I am loved; I am forgiven; I am accepted. I belong. I am not my own, because he has made me and he has redeemed me.

Nothing I can do or not do will change God's value system; only the righteousness of his son is acceptable before him, and he sees me in Christ. That frees me to be what I am: God's woman. That is my identity. I am his and he is mine. I am available to him, and he is available to me. This is the source of my security, and this is what frees me from the need to use others to validate me as a person.

What is true of me in my humanity is true of every other person. All are equal in accountability, spiritual responsibility, and the God-given freedom to choose. What is true of me as a child of God is true of every other child of God. The only distinguishing factor between the child of God and one who is not is redemption. Redemption is God's work, not mine.

The Christian view of equality is not political expediency, nor the battle between the sexes. (Competition and comparisons cannot co-exist with the spiritual principle of equality!) It is, rather, viewing ourselves and others from God's point of view.

We share God's creative expectations with all humanity. We need to see ourselves and others in terms of our mutual potential for becoming what God intended us to be—redeemed to himself.

The principle of equality reminds us that we all are sinners, all under pressure, feeling life's demands, and reacting accordingly. We need to develop an appropriate sensitivity to others' hurts—to weep with the weeping and rejoice with the rejoicing.

Christians mutually share the Holy Spirit and his gifts; therefore, we may and we must learn from everyone and anyone who is a believer. As 1 Corinthians 12 clearly teaches, we are a body made up of equally necessary members. "If one member suffers, all suffer together; if one member is honored, all rejoice together." Remembering it is *Christ's* body, we must make certain "that the members may have the same care for one another." And as James reminds us, we are to "show no partiality" as we "hold the faith of our Lord Jesus Christ, the Lord of glory" (James 2:1).

No one has arrived—we're all on a journey. We have a mutual destiny: to be conformed to the image of Christ—HIS image, not ours! This leaves no room for pedestals or for pariahs. We are to "Welcome one another, therefore, as Christ has welcomed you, for the glory of God" (Romans 15:7). We are not our own; we belong to the one who redeemed us. Herein lies the ground for acceptance of one another.

Each individual is—individual. Equality in value does not imply sameness. Each of us has the right to our own personhood. We must allow others that prerogative—even when it differs from ours! We are equal in value, but different in expression—sexually, culturally, racially, in the exercise of spiritual gifts and in personality variations.

"You shall have no other gods before me." "You shall not make for yourself a graven image, or any likeness of anything. You shall not bow down to them or serve them" (Exodus 20:3,4). This is phase one of God's program for human freedom. God is concerned with the true dignity and freedom of humanity. Since we are created as spiritual beings, one of the distinguishing features of our humanity is the need to worship. Though seemingly paradoxical, worship is really the key to our freedom. God seems to be saying, "Supplant me, sublimate me, and you will lose your ability to function as a whole human being. You will stymie your humanity."

Deuteronomy 30:6 says, "And the Lord your God will circumcise your heart and the heart of your offspring, so that you will love the Lord your God with all your heart and with all your soul, *that you may live*." The God who made us for himself is our First Cause and our First Love. We are to worship none but him. Surely this is not the least implication of our equality with all other persons. The very essence of sin is putting something finite before God. No one can serve two masters. Whatever honor and devotion we offer God is meaningless if at the same time there is a rival to him in our loyalty and affection. Actually, the rival to God is not others, but the self using others to sustain a sense of worth.

God's image in us gives equality of destiny and value. Any thought, act, or relationship which usurps his priority or authority in our lives is a false image. God is jealous of our commitment to him. He disallows false images because they engender false worship and nurture warped concepts of life, God, ourselves, and others. The effects of such twisted ideas, then, are perpetuated in offspring, home, church, and society. He is not jealous of us, but for us—on behalf of our blessedness, fulfillment, and wholeness.

The true image of God is the Person of the Lord Jesus Christ. The Apostle Paul tells us in Colossians 1:15, "He is the image of the invisible God, the first-born of all creation." And in the same chapter, Paul goes on to speak of "Christ in you, the hope of glory," and declares that our goal is "that we may present every man mature in Christ" (verses 27,28).

Our identity rests on this indwelling equality of Christ-in-you and Christ-in-me. We are not to imitate one another, but to reflect his life, in the context of our own individuality. You are a new creation; I am a new creation.

> From now on, therefore, we regard no one from a human point of view; even though we once regarded Christ from a human point of view, we regard him thus no longer. Therefore, if anyone is in Christ, he is a new creation; the old has passed away, behold the

new is come. All this is from God (2 Corinthians 5:16–18).

Both our expectations and our estimation of others,
as well as of ourselves, must now be reckoned from
Christ's vantage point. The old human value-system,
based on performance and prestige, is no longer apro-
pos. We will now see what God can do with a body
which has become the residence of the Holy Spirit, a
transformed mind and a "united" heart (Psalm
86:11).

6. *Contested Equality*

"And God said . . . have dominion . . . over every living thing. . . ." The dominion of man (male and female) gives purpose to the earth with all of its beauty and fruitfulness. Without humanity to appreciate and appropriate it, the earth would appear to be without significance. When mankind improperly controls the environment, the result is chaos and disaster. We were made to reign over the earth, to enjoy, appreciate, and maintain it, with sound judgment and commitment.

In a similar way, the dominion of God gives meaning to mankind. Godless philosophy deprives mankind of both meaning and worth. If our existence is traceable only to chance, we can destroy, or be destroyed without import. Why should issue be made of our rights as persons, our fulfillment and relationships, the structure of our society, if, indeed, we are creatures without design and destiny?

The revelation of the Scripture and a basic tenet of Christian faith is that earth was made for mankind, and mankind was made for God; that earth was made to serve us, and we, in turn, to serve God. In it all, God is the ultimate Resource. In all the universe he is the only no-need Being. We worship and serve him, not to meet his need but because to do so is appropriate and therefore fulfilling to our humanity.

In God's Manifesto of Human Liberty, the Ten Commandments, he clearly outlines the boundaries of our humanity, beginning with our need to worship only God, and describing appropriate human relational attitudes and actions. We learn that in giving to God first priority, every other relationship and commitment becomes an act of worship to him.

Worship is a human need, which is met only in the worship of God. Our equality with every other person makes it futile and meaningless to worship others or ourselves. Such misdirected worship is a refutation of our equality with others and our creature relationship with God.

Self-worship is god-playing. It is the human effort to simulate God's attributes. We imagine ourselves all-wise, all-powerful and perfect in performance. In this illusory frame of mind, we become demanding, domineering, manipulative, critical, aggressive, and possessive. And all of these are symptoms of our own insecurity, because when we try to be what we are not and what we cannot be, we hate ourselves; so that in the end we lose our sense of worth and identity.

God-playing has a predictable effect on our relationships with others. It produces defensiveness, abdication of responsibility, withdrawal, insecurity, hostility, bitterness, resentment, and sometimes even sexual deviations. God-playing is using others to accommodate to our ideals, tastes, physical and emotional needs; it is the vain attempt to find our identity in human relationships.

Aggression and dominance result from thinking we have rights over another. This too is a denial of our equality. Only God has prior claim over every person, male and female. We affirm our equality by recognizing God's prior claim in our lives as well as in others. Since we are mutually God's persons, we may not be possessive of one another. We are not to consume one another with self-interest, nor to exploit one another for selfish pleasure or prestige.

Each individual has the God-given freedom to make choices. We share this mutual responsibility and privilege with every other person. It is imperative that we respect that right. This disqualifies manipulating, domineering strategies. It is *God* who works in us, both to will and to do of *His* good pleasure. (*His* pleasure, *His* image, *His* work, not ours!) And He will continue to perform that work until the day of Jesus Christ (see Philippians 1:6).

Equal rights seem easy enough to work out on paper, but the simple fact is that none of us can maintain that perspective under the pressure of our own self-centered interests and demands. From that motivation our responses are confused and immature, with the result that we are both threatened and threatening. We fear exposure, rejection, and challenge, and we produce the same fear in others. Our equality is subject to competition, jealousy, and rivalry, as we vacillate between attitudes of inferiority and superiority.

But God has a plan for the survival of both our identity and our equality! Ironically, the very plan by which God intends to establish and mature us into whole and healed persons is the one which is misused and misinterpreted in such a way as to eventually destroy us. One way to test whether we have grasped God's loving and healing intent, and the perfection of his plan for us, is to simply state it as "headship–subjection" or "dominance–submission," and observe the emotional response!

If the words "submission" and "subjection" threaten our concept of identity, it is because we misunderstand the true implications of this God-given design. This negative, often hostile, response is culturally conditioned. We react to the *abuses* of God's design and therefore accept the connotation of injustice and inhumanity which those words have come to suggest.

Thus threatened, we may usurp the dominant–headship role, but there we sense the intolerable weight of responsibility, the exposure of our inadequacy and the contradiction to our basic femininity. We are uneasy and insecure in either role; neither seems suited to our human need, so we may settle into a medley of resentment or open hostility, pussycat manipulation, and power-plays, either overt or subtle.

In the male–female relationship, submission makes woman vulnerable, and thus becomes the means by which man is exposed as a tyrannical sinner or a redeemed lover. With Christ as the example, man is to serve the woman. As Christ's position was not jeopardized, neither will be the man's. Thus the headship–submission role becomes the test of mature manhood.

It is likewise the test of mature womanhood, by revealing the woman as either a manipulative sinner or a redeemed love-servant.

Every encounter between persons puts human equality under stress. If we are seeking to establish our identity in any role, or in any human relationship, we will always be threatened. And when we are threatened, we react in ways which threaten others. We must learn who we are in terms of who God is and what is his creative and redemptive purpose for us. If we fail to learn such an important truth, we will be insecure in any situation and in every relationship.

7. *The Dignity of Servanthood*

Who is this God whom we were made to serve? In Psalm 50:21 God says to one *alienated* from him, "You thought that I was one like yourself."

A true God does not exist unless he is a being apart from all other beings, unique and incomprehensible. In order to "know" him, we must begin by acknowledging that we cannot completely understand God. For in order to be God, he cannot in his essence be what we are. He is a being to be worshiped, with utter awe and reverence, before whom we realize the finiteness of our humanity. I cannot truly comprehend the significance of his love for me until I recognize that God is Love itself, infinite, eternal, all-encompassing LOVE. Only then will I know what it means to be loved. No human love can offer that—yet it is what I need. And only as I learn what it means to be so loved will I know what it means to be loving.

51

But how can we know this God whom we cannot understand? Since only God can know God, he must somehow be translated into terms we can comprehend. Nature tells us of his power and majesty, but though his character is attested to in the things which he has made, he is more than his creation. "God is spirit," Jesus tells us, "and those who worship him must worship in spirit and truth." We know then that the understanding of God must take place in the dimension of the spirit.

But God is a Person—a Person with whom we can relate as persons. This we know because he chose to reveal himself in the Person of the Lord Jesus Christ.

The fact of the incarnation of God in Jesus Christ is in itself unfathomable. We can scarcely comprehend, far less appreciate, the incredible fact that Christ Jesus our Lord who was the *morphe* of God, should CHOOSE TO SET ASIDE THAT IDENTITY, TAKING INSTEAD THE IDENTITY OF A SERVANT.

The Greek word *morphe,* used in Philippians 2:6, 7, translated "the form of," means the actual nature or essence subsisting in the individual and retained as long as the individual himself exists.

> Have this mind among yourselves, which you have in Christ Jesus, who, though he was in the form of God, did not count equality with God a thing to be grasped, but emptied himself, taking the form of a servant, being born in the likeness of men. And being found in human form he humbled himself and be-

came obedient unto death, even death on a
cross (Philippians 2:5–8).

Jesus Christ, though he could not in essence cease
to be God, deliberately chose the identity of a servant,
that he might subject himself in obedience to the will
of the Father, to the extent of dying on the cross! Oh,
that there were words to describe the magnitude of his
condescension, the venture of love, in this incomparable act of God!

We are not called upon to describe it in words, but
to live it. Herein is the very essence of the Christian
life. In his act of complete identification with us and the
giving up of his life on our behalf, God in the Person
of Jesus Christ, both set us the example and provided us
the means by which human beings may be redeemed
and live redemptively with one another.

Because God in Christ became one of us, setting aside
the prerogatives of his identity as God, in order to live
our life and die our death, we may enter his family as
beloved children. Infused once again with the life of
God we become temples in whom Christ himself dwells
to restore in us the image of God!

He who was God, emptied himself, humbled himself,
became obedient unto death, even death on a cross.
This he *chose* to do. And because he made this deliberate choice to set aside his own human will in order to
accede to the will of the Father ("Nevertheless, not
my will, but thine be done!") "God has highly exalted
him and bestowed on him the name which is above

53

every name, that at the name of Jesus every knee should bow, in heaven and on earth and under the earth, and every tongue confess that Jesus Christ is Lord, to the glory of God the Father" (Philippians 2:8–11).

In this is outlined for us a way of life unique in society, for we are exhorted to have this same mind-set in us, to do nothing from selfishness or conceit, but *in humility count others better than ourselves.* We are to look not only to our own interests but also to the interests of others, with the result of mutual exchange of encouragement in Christ—the fruits of which will be love, affection, sympathy, and full acknowledgment of the work of God's spirit in our lives.

What a beautiful picture of harmonious and fruitful relationships! How far removed from any suggestion of posturing, pretended humility, or of a pseudo-submission, submission which is simply a manipulative skill designed to accomplish our own ends. How totally different from a self-demeaning, repressive acquiescence, produced by fear or a faulty self-image.

This portrait of our Lord has all the elements of wholesome humanity, and contains all of the criteria by which we may test the authenticity of our own relatedness toward God and others. The Apostle Peter exhorts *all* Christians to servanthood, involving personal sacrifice and suffering, saying "For to this you have been called, because Christ also suffered for you, leaving you an example, that you should follow in his steps" (1 Peter 2:21). "By his wounds you have been healed," he tells us, and reminds us that this redemption found us "straying like sheep and returned us to the Shepherd and Guardian of our souls."

God, through Peter, uses the marriage relationship to illustrate the effectiveness of this kind of submissive attitude: A husband straying like a sheep, may be persuaded to return to his Shepherd by the reverent and chaste behavior of a wife whose spirit is subject to Christ. The healing of humanity was accomplished by the death and life of Christ Jesus who was willingly subject to the Father's purpose. This healing may be extended through us to the hurting, straying people around us, when we choose to make ourselves available to God's purpose for them.

By our Lord's example, we learn that a submissive spirit, a commitment to servanthood, must begin with a strong and authentic sense of identity. Jesus Christ was God; there was no doubt about the fact, nor was there any doubt of his awareness of the fact (John 10: 30). He, God the Son, was equal with God the Father. In the Godhead there exists perfect unity, oneness, and harmony.

However, seeing that we were helpless creatures lacking in ourselves the resources necessary to meet our needs, God elected to make himself available to humanity. How could God the Son, equal with God the Father, become his obedient servant? How could God become vulnerable to suffering and death? Only by choosing to become man, for man was designed to serve God. Only if he who never knew sin should choose to be sin, so that he could satisfy the penalty of our sin: death on a cross.

God did not pretend to become one of us; this was not Deity at play! This was God who is Love, loving. This was God at work to bring us to rebirth through his travail and agony. This was God the Son refusing to commute his right to be equal with God so that our needs might be met through his love-offering. Can we grasp it? In this supreme act of Love, God has told us that love knows no equal rights; that love's incentive makes possible a transfer of identity in which we become servants to one another deferring to one another's needs, giving priority to one another's interests. Willing to pluck out our eyes that others may see, to be the grain of wheat which dies redemptively.

The Apostle Peter, who enjoins us all to a life of servanthood, first establishes who we are:

> But you are a chosen race, a royal priesthood, a holy nation, God's own people
> . . . . Once you were no people, but now you are God's people; once you had not received mercy, but now you have received mercy (1 Peter 2:9,10).

"Live as free men . . . but live as servants of God," Peter says, for God's people have an identity which is secured by the character of God himself, and being a servant is no threat to that security. It is simply the means by which we may identify with Christ's own act of love, and so, Peter says, "Be subject for the Lord's sake . . . mindful of God . . . for God's approval."

The Apostle Paul speaks in concert with Peter:

> Therefore be imitators of God, as beloved children. And walk in love, as Christ loved us and gave himself up for us, a fragrant offering and sacrifice to God (Ephesians 5:1).

Then, having established who we are, and citing again the example of Christ himself, he says:

> Be subject to one another out of reverence for Christ (Ephesians 5:21).

And again, as various relationships are cited, the basis for subjection is Christ's example, our love-service to one another being "as servants of Christ," "as to the Lord" "rendering service with a good will, as to the Lord and not to men."

Christ's example also teaches us that authentic submission is not reluctant nor grudging, nor is it the result of imposed authority. It is rather a chosen, deliberate, voluntary, love-initiated response to another's need. It is an act of worship to God, whom we serve in serving others. In no way, then, is authentic submission a violation of our humanity. It is appropriate to the purpose for which we were created, since in serving his creatures we are serving and worshiping our Creator. And it acknowledges the dignity of our humanity because it is service freely rendered from a will surrendered to the loving purpose of God.

The world's list of great ones includes such as Napoleon, Lenin, Alexander, Machiavelli, the Lord Jesus Christ, through whom and for whom all things were created. (See Colossians 1:16.) Jesus says that those who humble themselves like children are greatest in his kingdom. He further tells us, "He who is greatest among you shall be your servant; whoever exalts himself will be humbled, and whoever humbles himself will be exalted" (Matthew 23:11,12). Peter and James both tell us that if we humble ourselves God will exalt us.

But, again, it is not a game. We are not to use humility to bargain for greatness, to look good in God's eyes or anyone else's. Humility happens to us when we least expect it and when we are least aware of it. It is the by-product of a realistic appraisal of who we are before God. It is in no way a denial of authentic personhood, since Christ Jesus sets the pattern for humility in his surrender to death. It is the absence of egocentricity, or self-centeredness; it is seeing ourselves and others from Christ's point of view. Humility is the attitude which motivates us to set aside our self-centered ambitions and desires in deference to God's work in both our lives and others', giving precedence to God's plan rather than our own. It is in this sense we "consider others better than ourselves." It is an affirmation of who we really are: God's own woman in whom neither conceit nor self-deprecation are appropriate.

Nor is humility a subtle way of patronizing people. There is no condescension in our identifying with another's need; temptation, trials, and failure are common to all—we are equally in need of forgiveness, mercy, love, and grace. Apart from the activity of God's Spirit, the human heart is far from altruistic. We serve in order to be served; we love in order to be loved; forgive in order to be forgiven. We may only serve with selflessness when we recognize ourselves as agents of God's activity, unable to initiate redemptive attitudes apart from him, but free to be godlike with God in control of both our willing and our doing.

Martin Luther said it so well: "A Christian is the

most free lord of all and subject to none; a Christian is the most dutiful servant of all and subject to everyone."

A free heart is one discharged of self-concern by the confidence that a loving Father-God is in control of all circumstances. A Father-God needing only the consent of our will to release the flow of his character through us making us adequate for every contingency of life. A spirit thus freed can respond, rather than react, to others. A strong sense of personhood comes from self-lessness rather than self-absorption. We find ourselves in losing ourselves because we were made to serve God not ourselves. When the focus of our thoughts and activities is on ourselves, we become neurotic in every dimension: physically, emotionally, and spiritually. But "losing" ourselves is not simply functional, it is a deliberate choice to follow our Lord's pattern, to set aside our rights (real or fancied), including equality with others, in favor of becoming expendable for Christ's sake—in the full dignity of Jesus' own incredible words: "But I am among you as one who serves!"

Servanthood, submission, humility! Three beautiful, healing, redemptive words. This is God's expedient for resolving the tensions in human relationships. And he, God, took his own medicine! Shall we obey this Lover of our souls?

8. *The Female Mode*

Why is the Statue of Liberty a woman rather than a man? Have you ever heard of Father Nature or Father Earth? Why are ships referred to in the feminine gender? Why do we instinctively refer to the delicately beautiful in nature as female, the sturdy and virile as male? And here on the peninsula, San Francisco is our city—we love her!

Throughout the Scriptures, symbols have consistent connotations, many of which are reflected in our literature as well as in the common vernacular. To some, the implications are threatening and demeaning; to others it is the acknowledgment of a unique mode of life as authentic and meaningful as maleness, but different in a way which is complementary to the other half of humanity.

Since the Scriptures constitute God's handbook for humanity, the consistency of its symbolism would appear to characterize the unique features of the sexes. On this premise, I offer the following sampler of feminine symbols in the Scriptures as a probable definition of the basic intent of femaleness.

The dove of peace has a biblical origin. The Genesis record of Noah and the ark pictures the patriarch using two birds to test post-flood conditions on the earth. "He sent forth a raven; and it went to and fro until the waters were dried up from the earth." "Then he sent forth a dove from him . . . but the dove found no place to set *her* foot." "He waited another seven days and again he sent forth the dove out of the ark; and the dove came back to him in the evening, and lo, in *her* mouth a freshly plucked olive leaf."

The dove is used in the New Testament to symbolize the Holy Spirit, as in the baptism of Jesus recorded in Matthew 3:16. The Holy Spirit (called the "Helper" in the New American Standard Version, John 15:26; compare "helper" Genesis 2:20) does not speak on his own initiative (NASV) or authority (RSV) Jesus tells us in John 16:13. It is the Holy Spirit's work to declare and clarify to us the work of Christ who is our peace. So, by illuminating the Person of Jesus Christ, the Holy Spirit becomes the instrument of peace in our lives.

A few years ago a man wrote an article in a leading magazine describing a women's meeting which began with hair-pulling and name-calling. He wrote with great sympathy for their frustration and their need to be recognized, and concluded by saying he felt women could be a great factor in bringing peace to the world if they were allowed a larger voice in political affairs!

It is my observation that the segments of society to which women have contributed the elements of peace have so benefited because those women were at peace, first of all, with themselves. A hostile, bitter spirit is as likely as a bayonet to produce peace. A gentle, quiet spirit, undemanding and unthreatening, is God's instrument to restore sanity and tranquillity in an angry world.

Freedom is also symbolized in the Scriptures by a woman. Galatians, chapter 4, uses Sarah, the free woman, to symbolize that "the Jerusalem above is free, and she is our mother." From the twenty-first chapter of Revelation we learn that "the holy city Jerusalem coming down out of heaven from God" is "the bride, the wife of the Lamb." The free woman, whose progeny is born of faith in God's promise, pictures the people of God. Among this people dwells the Lord God Almighty, the center of their worship, their eternal light and glory. In the worship of him and his redeeming grace, God's people become the matrix of true freedom to all who enter her fellowship by faith in her Lord.

On the other hand, Hagar, the slave woman, pictures the old Jerusalem—the center of the law. A people who, lacking experience of the delivering grace of God, are locked into a pattern of dead works. A woman in bondage thus becomes the symbol of the life lived apart from the redemption and resources of the living Christ.

Wisdom, in the Book of Proverbs, is personified as a

woman. Chapter nine says, "Wisdom has built her house, she has set up her seven pillars. She has slaughtered her beasts, she has mixed her wine, she has also set her table." Clearly, she is a woman of both strength and dignity, who by her own choice and initiative has established her personal identity (built her house) on the perfect righteousness of Christ (seven, the scriptural number of perfection; pillars, the firm foundation).

Wisdom understands that she must initiate the experience of forgiveness amplified in 1 John chapter 1, by: (1) walking in the light of God's truth, (2) expressing that truth in relationships with others, and (3) experiencing forgiveness and cleansing in the confession of sin thus exposed. In this way she "slaughtered her beasts," which is the allegorical statement of her personal appropriation of "the blood of Jesus Christ" or his atoning death.

"She has mixed her wine" symbolizes the joy with which her life is characterized, a joy resulting from a secure spiritual identity. A joy which she is eager to share with others. And so she sets her table to which others are invited:

> Come, eat of my bread
> and drink of the wine I have mixed.
> Leave simpleness, and live,
> and walk in the way of insight (Proverbs 9:5, 6).

Her life-message is extended through others, who take up the spirit and import of her godly perspective of herself and her freeing insights about life. A woman thus equipped for life is a living demonstration of the wisdom of God. *By her example* she initiates positive responses in others. Her life-style motivates others to live with freedom, joy, and dignity in the strength of a God-centered identity.

The woman whose life personifies wisdom knows that "The fear of the Lord is the beginning of wisdom, and the knowledge of the Holy One is insight." An example of this kind of applied-wisdom is cited by the Apostle Peter in his first letter, chapter 3, verse 1. Peter prefaces the ways in which believers are to live as servants of God in serving one another by saying:

> Having purified your souls by your obedience to the truth for a sincere love of the brethren, love one another earnestly from the heart (1 Peter 1:22).

The married woman, for instance, will motivate her husband to godliness by a life-style which speaks for itself, and does not need to be propped up with holy lectures and/or nagging and chiding.

From this we may see that wisdom, which is the subjective or practical side of knowledge, or objective truth, is functional in productive and healing relationships.

In Proverbs 9, the seductive woman, overt in her advances (she is noisy, wanton, shameless, she sits, she takes and she calls) initiates ungodly actions. Her life-message is a death sentence for those whom she motivates. There is neither wine nor blood in her personal identity, and therefore both joy and cleansing are absent from her relationships with others. She exploits them for personal gratification, and futility and death are the end product of her influence. Where there is no encounter with the atoning death of Christ, no experience of the joy of his living Presence, there is no spiritual identity, no personal fulfillment. There is no recourse to the "mind of Christ," the wisdom from above, and the resulting insecurity is evident in fraudulent relationships.

"Wisdom builds her house, but folly with her own hands tears it down" (Proverbs 14:1). A woman who relates to life with godly wisdom is establishing a secure identity. Anything less is self-destructive.

Repeatedly, the Old Testament prophets, calling God's recalcitrant, disobedient nation to repentance, referred to her as an unfaithful wife, a harlot. In her exile she has widowed her mother city. The daughter of Zion has departed all her majesty. The Lord has trodden as in a wine press the virgin daughter of Judah. She is a maiden whose lovers cannot comfort her. The epitome of spiritual unfaithfulness is the great harlot of Revelation, "who corrupted the earth with her fornication."

On the other hand, the new humanity, God's chosen and redeemed society, the church, is referred to as the Bride of Christ, the wife of the Lamb, a bride adorned for her husband. She is clothed with fine linen, bright and pure . . . the righteous deeds of the saints (Revelation 19:7,8). Again, the holy city Jerusalem, coming down out of heaven from God, is pictured as the Bride, the wife of the Lamb, having the glory of God, with radiance like a most rare jewel, like a jasper, clear as crystal (Revelation 21:9–11). Again we are reminded of 1 Peter 3:3–5, and the woman there described as gentle and quiet in spirit, which attitude is said to be an imperishable jewel which in God's sight is very precious!

With superb poetic grace, the Song of Solomon depicts the love relationship between Christ and his Bride. The sensuous aspects of human love are used to depict the existential quality of God's relationship with his own people. This book, as perhaps no other passage of Scripture, teaches clearly the harmony of the spiritual with the emotional and physical aspects of our humanity. There is nothing here of the so-called "puritanical" view of sex, in which the physical act itself is considered impure. It depicts the beauty of a pure love between a man and a woman, which ripens into an undying mutual devotion. It is a highly poetic picture of the full implications of pure and sacred love and marriage.

In it all, we are taught that the source of all true love is God. He is Love. We are taught that he made us for himself, in order to make us the objects of his infinite and unequivocal love—the love which constrained him to die for his beloved.

The Apostle Paul expounds the message of the Song of Solomon in Ephesians 5:22–33. The teaching on headship and submission in the marriage relationship must be seen as the corollary to the theology of Ephesians. He begins with phrases so rich in spiritual romance that heart and mind fairly burst with ecstasy.

Then he enjoins us to "walk in love, as Christ loved us and gave himself up for us, a fragrant offering and sacrifice to God" (5:2). And then, acknowledging the "great mystery" of the marriage union, he relates it to the union between Christ and the church, which is depicted by the headship of the husband and the submission of the wife—all in the context of God relating to his people through the Lord Jesus Christ. No one, surely *no one* who understands the spiritual implications, the love commitment of the believer with Christ, could accuse the Apostle Paul of chauvinism in such a context!

Peace, freedom, wisdom, beauty, fidelity, love—all are symbolized in the female gender. Are they then exclusively female characteristics? Of course not! But may it be that the godly woman, whose gentle, quiet spirit is her love-response to God's loving authority, in a unique way releases others to understand and experience these qualities of life. Is it not possible that the woman who responds with wise and loving submission to the authority of her husband might set him free to headship in the home? And this headship would, if universally practiced, set in motion a cycle of redemptive social responses which would restore order and love to humanity.

In a deep, insightful article in *Harper's* magazine, July, 1973, entitled "The Suicide of the Sexes," George Gilder makes some extraordinarily perceptive comments on the implications of sexuality in society. He articulates the disastrous results to society of minimizing sexual differences, and states that "sexual energy animates most of our activities and connects every individual to a family and a community, and through these to a past and a future." He further states that "sexuality is best examined not as sexology, physiology, or psychology, but as a study encompassing all the deepest purposes of a society."

With persuasive clarity he reasons that "males are the sexual outsiders and inferiors," who without long-term commitments to and from women—without the institution of marriage—are exiles from the procreative chain of nature. "From almost the start," he says, "the boy's sexual identity is dependent on acts of exploration and initiative." These he feels are less vital to a woman, whose sexual identity is stamped in her very being, or patently obvious in her anatomy, even though she may fail to bear children.

While the views expressed by Mr. Gilder in this article are from a secular viewpoint, I see them as strongly supportive of the necessity for the traditional and scriptural female role of nurturer and motivator. If, indeed, the male is insecure in his sexuality and therefore afloat in his social identity, female dominance can only heighten his sense of uncertainty and dispossess society of maleness. On the other hand, a woman, being secure in her sexual identity, can support maleness by developing in man a sense of headship responsibility. Such a woman can secure to society the love, intimacy, and companionship of marriage and the family by validating the man as father and provider.

Submission is a subtle and sensitive role in human

relationships. Apart from a secure spiritual identity, it will be seen as a threat to personal autonomy. With her God-given sensitivity and a will subject to his loving wisdom, a woman can, by her example, teach this healing, cohesive principle to husband, family, church, and society. Will we relinquish this privilege and responsibility to a self-centered insistence on our rights? May we allow God to free us from bondage to ourselves and extend that liberty of spirit through us to others!

9. *Woman in Eden (Part 1)*

As we noted earlier, the first mention of a male–female creation in the Scriptures confirms that, (1) both were created in the image and likeness of God; (2) both were given dominion over the earth and every living thing on the earth; (3) both were given the command to "be fruitful and multiply, and fill the earth and subdue it"; and (4) God provided sustenance for all of his creation.

Since both male and female were made in the image and likeness of God, each was equipped for spiritual autonomy, under their Creator, and within the purpose of God. He vested in each the faculty for making moral choices; this differentiated humanity from beast. Genesis 1:1 through 2:4 is the summary of creation. In it there is no suggestion of differences between man and woman.

Genesis 2:4b through 25 is the detailed account of

the creation of man and woman, and this passage is critical to the understanding of our sexuality. Jesus and Paul both derive their teaching on sexual relationships in marriage, the church, and society from this body of truth. A careful and reverent scrutiny of it is imperative. The following is offered in the hope it will serve as a catalyst to a more profound investigation, by and for both men and women. It will be an attempt to ferret out some of the subjective truth of the passage, to complement the usual more objective teaching of this and other related passages.

The opening chapters of Genesis are archetypal; that is, they are the predecessor of future events. Thus, we find ourselves continually involved in the creative process, constantly confronted with the issue of sexuality, besieged with satanic efforts to delude us, preying on our own yen to play God. As it was in the beginning, so it continues to be.

God must be the Initiator of every act, of every thought, of Life and Love and Truth. The Book of Revelation tells us that he is the alpha and the omega. Revelation 21:5 says, "And he who sat upon the throne said, 'Behold, I make all things new.'" And Paul states, "Therefore, if any one is in Christ, he is a new creature; the old has passed away, behold the new has come. All this is from God . . ." As in the beginning, God brings order out of chaos, gives beauty for ashes, frees us for creative adventure.

Who is your first-love?
the one who makes you feel really honestly you,

with whom time spent is quality time,
who brings to your life renewal and dimension,
   beauty and wholeness
who recognizes the uniqueness of your potential
   and fully respects your humanity
who is willing to share your joys and distresses
   and forgive your failures
      with undaunted acceptance
whose love holds you captive, yet sets you free
who would die for you or live for you,
   and who evokes the same response from you
who thus teaches you to love and to be loved.
Is anything less than this really love?
Is there really anything more
   than Agape Himself?
Who alone has earned the right to be our
   First-love!

In the first chapter of Genesis our mutual identity is defined. Since God is both sovereign and immutable, I believe it is not only possible but necessary to see the harmony in his creative intent in both chapters two and three. When God's prescribed order seems dysfunctional, it is never due to a flaw in his design, but to our faulty understanding and consequent misuse of his workmanship. Cultural conditioning includes both cumulative error and a racial memory of God's directive for our humanity and our sexuality. Our minds and hearts are cluttered with inherited and personally acquired debris. The integrity of God's character and of the Scriptures themselves assures to us the only source of pure truth. It is appropriate to approach the Scriptures with awe and humility, so that our "faith might not rest in the wisdom of men but in the power of God" (1 Corinthians 2:5).

I believe the order in which the creation story is told is significant in delineating the difference between identity and function; that is, it seems evident that chapter one is the summary of our human identity, while chapters two and three detail our sexual function. The dignity and precision of these passages must not be questioned. As I once heard Dr. Arthur Custance remark, "This is a child's story only if a child is reading it." We will want childlike faith in the God who made us, and a mature understanding of his intent, both of which are gifts of his Spirit.

We will first need to observe, as does the Apostle Paul in 1 Corinthians 11:8, that man was created before woman. And now we must ask ourselves some serious questions. I believe they are questions which need to be considered individually, as men and as women, and corporately, as society in general and the church specifically.

Unique to our humanity is our need to worship, which is designed to be directed to God. When it is misdirected, to ourselves or another human, we involve ourselves with feelings of superiority and inferiority. In their original, sinless state, the first man and woman were unthreatened by the order of their creation. There was harmony, openness, and unbroken fellowship between them and with God. This was to last as long as the order of worship was not violated.

Women react defensively to the order of creation

because men, acting out of self-worship, have assumed that priority means preeminence. This is threatening to a woman who has a self-worship program of her own. We will need to examine together the reasons for our emotional responses to the sequence in creation.

There exists a need to consider the related issue of the Creator's prerogative, to ask ourselves the penetrating questions: Am I willing to allow God to be God? Do I really believe that God made me to be loved and to be loving? Do I view the sequence of creation as a threat to human equality? Am I committed to finding God's intention, setting aside personal and social prejudices, believing that the will of God is good and acceptable and perfect? Do I understand that deteriorated relationships are not a result of God's design, but a result of mankind's refusal to follow that design?

I believe the order of creation for man and woman suggests God's intended order of government for the family unit, and that this order has extended implications in the church and society as a whole.

The freedom to make choices is a basic element of our humanity, this element affects all of our relationships. It also involves an individual responsibility for the implications of choices we make. In the ultimate, however, God himself assumes the responsibility for our choices, both individually and for all humanity. The cross of Christ is proof that God has taken on himself the ultimate responsibility for our malignant choices.

Implicit in every social structure is the need for

both the individual freedom to choose and to assume responsibility for the results of choosing. The essential difference between anarchy and government is that in the latter responsibility for certain corporate choices is sustained by a select few. This necessitates trust, and a willingness to relinquish some amount of personal autonomy. Here again we find the conflict of interest, the inferiority-superiority struggle, the power plays, the identity crises, and always for the same reason: the misdirected use of the freedom to choose—focused on self-centered interests rather than the common good. Or, to put it the other way, self-worship rather than God-worship, since he is the one who can best determine and define the common good.

On the whole, society recognizes the necessity for government in every social unit, as an arbiter of choices and a focus for responsibility. The teaching of the Apostle Paul is that "there is no authority except from God, and those that exist have been instituted by God" (Romans 13:1). I believe Genesis 1–3 records the earliest governmental forms, instituted by God, defining the basic principles for all authority structure.

This authority structure begins with God who creates, and orders his creation. Man and woman, as spiritual beings, are equally responsible to God. This authority structure might be seen as an isosceles triangle, with God at the apex. Our equality as persons, established in Genesis, chapter one, is reaffirmed in chapter two where we see that God formed each as a unique creation, giving each time to relate to him alone. Adam was anesthetized during Eve's creation!

And to make certain that Adam would understand the equal status of the woman, God gave him the demanding task of naming the beasts and birds. This necessitated a complete familiarity with the character of these creatures. What an ingenious method for distinguishing his own humanity and establishing his need for a suitable counterpart, "a helper fit for him." A helper sharing his bone and his flesh, and above all the image of God!

Clearly, Adam recognized his dependence upon the Lord God, who had given him life and everything needed to sustain it. God had put him in the garden in Eden, and there had planted for him "every tree that is pleasant to the sight and good for food, the tree of life also in the midst of the garden, and the tree of the knowledge of good and evil" (Genesis 2:8, 9). In denying him access to the latter, God was providing him opportunity to validate his humanity by freely choosing to submit to God's authority. Adam owed his life and sustenance to God's initiative and design, and God gave him the purpose for which to live. He was to cultivate, possess and enjoy the resources which God had provided, expressing in his activity the character of God. He was a man under orders. He was also a man on whom God had lavished tender, loving care, a man designed to be, under God, the head of the race.

But there was no counterpart to his humanity, no complement to his maleness. There was no one with whom he could interact, with whom he could express the potential godlikeness for which he had been created.

> Then the Lord God said, "It is not good that the man should be alone; I will make him a helper fit for him" (Genesis 2:18).

In Hebrews 13:6 we are told that "we can confidently say, 'The Lord is my helper, I will not be afraid.' " By what strange twist of perspective can women on one hand joyfully claim the Lord as our helper and disclaim as though it were a dishonor the position of helper to man? I think we do have here a case of cultural conditioning! Ought we not rather be awed that God has chosen for us to relate to man in the same way he does? I suggest this is a test of a godly versus worldly perspective of the woman's function. It also tests whether we function as God's woman, secure in our spiritual identity, or in dependence upon human approval.

Following each stage of creation we read "and God saw that it was good." Everything but Adam was in its own way appropriate to God's workmanship. But man was made in God's image, and God is a union of three Persons in One. "Let *us* make man in *our* image, after *our* likeness" (Genesis 1:26). It was God's plan to reveal himself to his creation through *relationships!* God was initiating a family, named Man (note, this is the name *God* gave us, Genesis 5:2). It was "not good" that man should be alone because God's will, by which "good" is defined, could not be consummated without

the woman. And, to state it tirelessly, God's will was
to express his character through the male–female humanity, to whom he gave authority to have dominion
over the earth and every living thing on the earth and
to be fruitful and multiply, filling and subduing the
earth. Multiplied relationships—expanded opportunity for adventure and loving conquest of a richly
endowed environment!

This is the context in which God sets in complement the headship responsibility of the male and the
sensitive-support responsibility of the female. Each is
supportive of the other in a unique way. The man
takes the governmental responsibility ("the buck
stops on his desk"), the woman supports him, with
wisdom and trust. Or, as the Apostle Paul puts it in
1 Corinthians 11:11, 12:

> (Nevertheless, in the Lord woman is not
> independent of man nor man of woman; for
> as woman was made from man, so man is
> now born of woman. *And all things are from
> God.*)

It is not, then, a matter of comparing "rights," but of
seeing the privilege and responsibility of functioning
in the uniqueness of our individuality according to
God's design. Outside of this design we all are misfits.

Genesis 2:22–25 records the first union of a man
and woman in a marriage ceremony performed by
God. Suppose it could be said of every marriage, "the
Lord God . . . made . . . a woman and brought her
to the man!" Suppose the prerequisite to marriage

were a woman made whole and beautiful by her encounter with the living God, led by him to a man
"under orders" and equipped for life because of his
communion with his Creator! It would have a profound effect upon the joy and spiritual quality of that
union. And I daresay it would change considerably
the common mode of courtship which we as a society
have taught our young. Well might such a man respond to such a woman with the words of Adam: "This
at last is bone of my bone and flesh of my flesh." (One
student of Hebrew tells me the words "at last" are the
equivalent to the modern term "WOW!") The quality of such a God-ordained union would form the
prospectus for a three-dimensional unity which would
glorify the God who united them. The isosceles triangle is completed in the union of man and woman
equal in identity, complementary in function, in harmony with one another because God is preeminent in
their lives.

Interestingly, to this point the words "adam" and
"man" are used interchangeably, taken from the Hebrew root which simply refers to the earth from which
the man was created, a common nonspecific reference
to a man. In verses 23 and 24 the Hebrew idiom
changes to indicate a special nobility, power of will,
individuality, the word "Ish" of which the feminine
"Ishah" is the diminutive. And so "God saw everything that he had made, and behold, it was very good!"

In his article, "The Suicide of the Sexes," George
Gilder describes what he refers to as "a man's predica-
ment" from his earliest years to manhood, affirming

his sexuality first through his mother, then his father, to then become, without the "civilizing effect" of marriage and family, predatory in sexual exploits and economics. Can it be, Mr. Gilder, that God anticipated the problem in the "simple" solution of Genesis 2:24, "Therefore, a man leaves his father and his mother and cleaves to his wife, and they become one flesh"? Therefore . . . supported by this new "thou" relationship, with new validation and strength for his authority, the man leaves his old authority structure, his old system for social security, to establish a stronger union in which his headship is affirmed in the context of spiritual equality.

They were both naked, and were not ashamed. They had both self-awareness and other-awareness, but without self-centeredness. The crux of their commitment was God himself, and in the pristine beauty of that threefold relationship they were secure, unthreatened and unthreatening. Having studied neither Freud nor Skinner they knew who they were and why they were there. God had taught them their life philosophy and given them their life-message. He synthesized their psycho-sexual behavior and harmonized their polarities. There were no hidden subtleties or programmed strategies, no vying for rights or dominance, because God was the resolution to their identity, the motivation for their function . . . "for such a harmony could not exist, except they all consented to some one end" (George Macdonald in *Phantastes*).

A transparent, open, and guileless relationship was the result of their submission to his loving authority, under which they were totally free to be fully human. There was neither exploitation nor intimidation in the God-ordained authority structure: God, the First Cause, to whom each was individually responsible— the man for loving headship, the woman for supportive submission. Man, to convey the glory of God to woman, woman to display the glory of God for man.

Thus marriage, instituted by God from creation, becomes the spool from which is woven the fabric of all relationships. From it we are to learn the principles of unity, fidelity, commitment, authority, submission, and love as an expression of worship to God. Marriage is not the end in itself, but a means by which we demonstrate the strong and tender love of the Creator-God, a God fiercely jealous for the true good which brings delight and fulfillment to every facet of our humanity. A God of law and order by which he channels to us "the sweet air blowing from the land of righteousness," in whose garden we may freely eat of every tree that delights and satisfies our deepest needs.

In marriage we are to see God relating to his people, Christ relating to his church, and in it all how humanity functions in terms of the indwelling life of Jesus Christ, who is the express image of the Father. In this way marriage sets the principles, the pattern, for all human relationships, for in them all we relate as sexual beings, according to our God-assigned function.

10. *Woman in Eden (Part 2)*

Since the direction our lives take and the influence we have upon others is determined by the choices we make, it is crucial for us to be able to define good and evil. The human view is that everything conforming to my ideas and wishes, is good, and of course everything not conforming is bad. The name for this system of thought is humanism. And from this viewpoint, God is either non-existent, threatening, or controllable. The Apostle Paul labels this the "natural mind," and apart from Jesus Christ, that is the mindset of the human race (Romans 7:15 ff.). It is the human "good" which results in evil. We are four billion egocentrics, competing for first place. The result is war, chaos, divorce, ulcers, loneliness, bitterness, bigotry, etc.

The solution even a child can comprehend. One day our daughter, Laurie, then five years old, brought a tearful report of conflict between a playmate and herself. We talked it over, applying the old biblical principle of the mote and the beam, allowing the Spirit of God to correct our thinking, and giving time for the emotions to adjust to that reality. Then Laurie said, "Mother, isn't it a good thing we have God, or how would we know good from bad?" I have never been able to state it so well!

God is good, and goodness is godlikeness. That is the only no-contest criterion for goodness. In God's Person there is an inflexible, impeccable Good which transcends law, but which every just law tries to preserve. This is the Life of God, the Life which may be described as LOVE and JOY and PEACE. It is the life he created us to live, but which cannot be lived apart from him, and therefore depends upon an unbroken relationship with him, a relationship of love and trust.

For every positive there is a negative. One wonders whether a positive can exist as such without its negative. Thus, God who is Love can hate evil, be jealous for the good of his people and be provoked to wrath by defiant, rebellious sinners. (A wrath which he turned on himself in Jesus Christ who became sin for us and paid the price of our rebellion!) It appears then that the very existence of good poses the potential for the existence of evil—not, however, a negative which harmonizes and accentuates a positive, but a defiant opposition to that which is good, a negative gone hostile and asserting itself as Good.

The Lord God commanded the man (thereby making him governmentally responsible) to not eat of the tree of the knowledge of good and evil, warning him "in the day that you eat of it you shall die." Physical death was, of course, imminent in choosing to disobey, but of far greater import was the effect of death upon the whole person—death to the spirit and death to the soul. In knowing good, Adam would think himself Good, and, setting himself up as God, become evil. Thinking himself Love, rather than Love's agent, he would lose the faculty for loving; thinking himself Joy, rather than the agent of God's Joy, he would no longer experience joy. Claiming to be wise, he would become a fool, futile and senseless in his view of God and of himself (Romans 1:18–32).

God, who is Good, is a Person. The first man and woman had communion with him. He had shared his creative plan with them and infused and surrounded them with his life, including the tree of life "in the midst of the garden."

Evil is also a person, and Satan is his name. (Incidentally, if we object to the masculine pronoun for God, should we not also protest the masculine pronoun for Satan?) Although there is evil in our nature, humanity of itself is neither Good nor Evil; we may opt for the control of either, and in either case we are dealing with a person, God or Satan.

Satan's stock in trade is subtlety. In Revelation 12:9 he is referred to as "the deceiver of the whole world." The Hebrew word from which the translation "the serpent" is made, actually means "the shining one." Second Corinthians 11:14, 15 says, ". . . for even Satan disguises himself as an angel of light. So it is not strange if his servants also disguise themselves as servants of righteousness." He is an artist in craftiness and deception, in the distortion of truth, and *he is behind* all deceitful strategy, the model for all pretense. "*I will make myself* like the Most High," was the exalted boast which articulated his absolute commitment to evil (Isaiah 14:12–14). His outward beauty was a veil for inward corruption, a trap for the easily deceived.

Satan, the subtle strategist, made his initial appeal to the woman. He did not go to the governmental head of the race, but took his appeal to "the people." I believe Satan's choice of the woman strongly suggests that he understood the distinctiveness of the male–female function and characteristics. Would the subtle deceiver choose to "lay it on" the less subjective, more judicially culpable of the two? Would he not find it strategically expeditious to aim at the man through the woman, particularly if she were the way to the man's heart? Certainly the tactic of a subtle enemy bent on subversion and exploitation would be to attack at the point of greatest vulnerability.

And yet, characteristics which accompany vulnerability are those which we highly esteem, such as a keen sensitivity and a faculty for adapting to life and people. We admire one who can motivate with gentleness and compassion. These are the characteristics of the emotionally strong and mature. But the temperament from which these strengths may spring can also produce an inversion to these strengths, by virtue of its vulnerability. It may be well to remind ourselves at this point that in the discussion of temperamental and biological differences, we are not at all addressing the question of identity or worth, but only a variety in function.

Nor are we attempting to put an either-or characterization to the male and female, but rather a more-less distinction. Obviously, we may not say woman is sensitive, man is insensitive; woman is illogical, man is logical. We are a long way from the original creation, and each of us is a complicated structure of genes and culture. But just as the male–female biological pattern has remained irreversible, so I believe has the basic structure of the male–female psyche instituted by our Creator. This is why I believe we must listen so carefully to these Genesis passages, comparing them with the whole body of Scripture.

There is in all of us the racial memory of Eden, when we were like God, made in his image, where two human wills were harmonized in the full expression of humanity through choosing to relate to God on his terms. God had given Adam and Eve a loaded option: "every tree that is pleasant to sight and good for food, and the tree of life also in the midst of the garden," with only one prohibition. The key issue was obedience, their will subject to God's will.

We live each day between Eden and heaven, under attack from an enemy who introduces doubt and distrust of God and one another through deceit and subtlety. God is not enough, the enemy suggests, or God is dispensable. You have what it takes to go it alone, or at least to make a good show. Then we take off on our self-centered excursions, and my way versus God's way becomes my way versus yours. When we transfer our faith and our expectations from God to ourselves or others, we breed fantasy, illusion, frustration and despair. No human being can fulfill himself or another except in a secondary manner as an agent of God's life, filled with the character of the indwelling Jesus Christ, taught and empowered by His Spirit. "We have this treasure in earthen vessels, that the surpassing greatness of the power may be of God and not from ourselves" (2 Corinthians 4:7).

God has given us all of life to enjoy, but that enjoyment is contingent upon his control of our motivation; that is, the control of agape Love, a love which is always satisfied because it demands no gratification from the loved object. God who is *agape* Love is its only Source. Without him, human "loves" are at best a shabby imitation, at worst a devastating tyranny, and in either case a diversion from the Giver. Controlled by *agape* Love, we are free to enjoy every relationship without emotional sabotage, and in it we are always drawn back to the Giver. God's image is restored in us when he is in control of our human faculties.

An independent identity is an illusion. We simply choose the form of government under which we shall live, God's or Satan's. Our emerging function will be good or evil, accordingly. God tells us truth about ourselves and life; Satan offers a counterfeit, and his initial thrust is an attack upon God's credibility. To question God's character is to question his very existence. When we face our doubts to the dregs we are brought to the unbearable conclusion of godlessness, and then, because we were made to be possessed by God, we will choose to return to him, or we will opt for a counterfeit.

The woman met the enemy alone, and she was no match for his subtlety. The Apostle Paul uses the Greek word *exapatao,* to indicate intensive deception (1 Timothy 2:14). She violated her unity with God and with the man, and, unsupported, she bought the twisted perversion in which Satan offered her godlike-ness. Deluded into thinking God had cramped her style, deprived her of her rights, she defied his authority, "took of the fruit and ate." Then, deeply engaged in the satanic enchantment she offered the fruit to the man.

The Holy Spirit through the Apostle Paul tells us Adam was not deceived (and here the milder word, *apatao,* is used). The man, without recourse to God, and in full possession of his objective capacities, capitulated to the woman, "and he ate."

> Then the eyes of both were opened, and they knew that they were naked; and they sewed fig leaves together and made themselves aprons (Genesis 3:7).

The psycho-sexual-spiritual implications of this account are profound. In it we are taught the basic format for human existence, the struggle between God and Satan, the function of choosing. The deepest issues of our sexuality are implicit in these "simple" phrases, if we will be teachable and transparently honest with ourselves and the Spirit of God.

I believe it consistent with the entire body of Scripture to define sin as placing something or someone finite before God. Satan, appearing in beautiful guise, first engaged the woman's emotions; then with seeming logic he persuaded her that she could add dimension to her humanity beyond the limits proscribed by God and on her own initiative. She could be godlike without God, and she would share her new, independent adequacy with the man. She would offer him more than God, and, by-passing him, she would be man's Help, rather than his helpmate, his First Cause rather than his supporter (or to put it in the language of some contemporary literature), "the idol of her husband's heart." "Godplaying," we sometimes call it; "idolatry," is God's name for it.

Adam met the woman alone, and he was no match for her. First Timothy 2:14 tells us he was not deceived, and later he would respond to God's questioning by blaming "the woman whom thou gavest to be with me." We are not told her method. Did she nag, wheedle, weep, threaten, bribe, tease, or all of same? Or perhaps she feigned submission—the subtlest weapon of all. At any rate, Adam, out on a limb ignoring God, surrendered his headship, and "sin came into the world through one man" (Romans 5:12).

The Genesis reference to nakedness is solid confirmation of the synthesis of body, soul, and spirit in humanity. Our first ancestors were at peace with their bodies so long as they were in unbroken unity with God. Sin had not yet defiled their humanity and so their nakedness was not an issue. And since their relationship with God was unbroken, and their identity therefore unthreatened, they had no need to mask their humanity nor to support it with contrived trappings. There was no shame because there was no guilt.

The moment they committed themselves to their own defiant method for understanding good and evil, guilt enveloped their entire persons. The sexual polarities which had once been harmonized and complemented in spiritual unity with God and each other, now became an embarrassment. Now alienated from God, they become defensive, self-centered, and seek ways to hide from him and from one another.

With simple elegance, the story of our lives:

> And they heard the sound of the Lord God walking in the garden in the cool of the day, and the man and his wife hid themselves from the presence of the Lord God among the trees of the garden (Genesis 2:8) .

With poignant beauty, the story of humanity's Lover, the Hound of Heaven:

> But the Lord God called to the man, and said to him, "Where are you?" (Genesis 2:9) .

Again, God initiates the encounter with Adam, the head of the race, holding him responsible to the divine commandment; a commandment which, if observed, would have interpreted their freedom and delivered them from the bondage of self-centeredness. And now the question which will incriminate the woman as his motivator as Adam evades his responsibility: "Who told you that you were naked? Have you eaten of the tree of which I commanded you not to eat?" (Genesis 2:11).

Eden's Watergate unfolds, with cross accusations, buck-passing and the fading fig leaves of unrepentant self-righteousness. Adam blames the woman, and God for giving her to him. The woman cites the beguiling serpent.

And God? Once they knew him as their Creator-Lover. Now they will know him as their Lover-Redeemer!

11. *God's Survival Plan*

Genesis 3:14–24 is sometimes referred to as "the curse." Read without negative preconditioning, it is evident that the curse was addressed to the serpent and to the ground; it was not applied to the man or the woman. Actually, God instituted a new regime at this time which would protect us from ourselves. For the woman, he reinforced the authority needed to shield her in her female vulnerability. To the man he gave the therapy and discipline of work. In it all, God revealed the way in which the tensions between good and evil would be resolved within his own redemptive plan. A word from Dorothy L. Sayers will be helpful here:

> God did not abolish the fact of evil: He transformed it. He did not stop the crucifixion: He rose from the dead.

In the spirit of Jesus' own words: "For God sent the

Son into the world, not to condemn the world, but that the world might be saved through him," we have in this Genesis passage not a condemnation of God's creation, but a plan for its redemption. It is well to remind ourselves that it simply will not do to be defensive with God. He is not the enemy; we are. He only *seems* our enemy when we oppose him, and in resisting him we oppose ourselves.

This Genesis passage is both prescription and description; that is, in it the Lord God is prescribing the cure to conflict as well as tracing the course of human relationships. He begins by addressing evil personified in the serpent, and, to symbolize its humiliating defeat, sentences it to crawling on its belly, eating dust. And dust is humanity without the life of God. We are vulnerable to evil only when apart from Him. Satan brought off his great con of the woman when she met him alone; Adam surrendered the integrity of his headship when he encountered the woman alone. The race fell in Adam, who chose to be motivated by the woman, who chose to be motivated by the serpent, who usurped God's prerogative to motivate his people to work for his good pleasure (Philippians 2:13).

Now God reinstates the order of headship by declaring an end to the coalition between the serpent and the woman, exposing him as a figure-head, and declaring open warfare between the two:

> Then the Lord God said to the woman, "What is this that you have done?" The woman said, "The serpent beguiled me, and I ate." The Lord God said to the serpent,

"Because you have done this, cursed are you
above all cattle, and above all wild animals;
upon your belly you shall go, and dust you
shall eat all the days of your life. I will put
enmity between you and the woman, and
between your seed and her seed; he shall
bruise your head, and you shall bruise his
heel" (Genesis 3:13–15).

What blind unbelief, what satanic delusion, has
prevented us from seeing the tender love, the forgiving
grace of God restoring the woman to dignity and worth
as the means by which he would enter the stream of
humanity and purify it with his redeeming death and
life? The promised seed of the woman who would
conquer Satan is the Son of God, the Lord Jesus Christ,
born of Mary, the virgin—born of *woman!* No, God
did not condemn the woman; he forgave her, restored
her perspective and reinstated her to the security of
his loving authority. Another day, Jesus would extend
such mercy to a woman taken in adultery: " . . . neither do I condemn you! Go, and sin no more."

In a world rampant with chaos, childbirth can seem
futile, if not disastrous, to human reasoning. If life is
a tyrannical trap, a futile maze of meaningless choices,
then the biological function of producing another
human being is without significance. Extinction becomes the preferred alternative to functioning as a
"baby machine," and thus perpetuating the human
tragedy.

It becomes a question of sheer faith. Either we believe in the answers or non-answers of science and

philosophy and react inevitably with despair or we must believe that God is "nearer to us than breathing, closer than hands and feet," and that this personal God is in sovereign control of human affairs.

This personal, sovereign God addresses the woman. This time he addresses her first. One reason is that the topic is now God's redemptive plan in which woman will figure prominently as the instrument of the Incarnation. Only the redemptive intervention of God in Jesus Christ will give significance and meaning to the survival of the human race, and dimension, therefore, to motherhood.

But we so easily forget that life is a fragile and precious gift from God, that the act of procreation is a serious and sensitive function of our humanity necessitating godly wisdom and perspective. "Thou didst knit me together in my mother's womb," is the reverent declaration of the psalmist, giving the dimension of worship to the function of reproduction. This worship acknowledges that in it all God is at work to bring order and meaning to life. In *The Problem of Pain*, C. S. Lewis says, "God whispers to us in our pleasures, speaks in our conscience, but shouts in our pains; it is his megaphone to rouse a deaf world." The pain of childbirth, and indeed of child-rearing, is divinely designed to draw us back to the source of Life and Love and Wisdom without which we flounder hopelessly in our inadequacy. If the hand that rocks the cradle rules the world, then global redemption of motherhood is long overdue and we need desperately to return that rule to the hand of our Creator-Father, so that we in turn may learn of him what our intended functioning is and be fulfilled in it.

> To the woman he said, "I will greatly multiply your pain in childbearing; in pain you shall bring forth children, yet your desire shall be for your husband, and he shall rule over you" (Genesis 3:16,17).

The Lord God now gives the therapy, creativity and discipline of work to both the woman and the man, but in different contexts, consistent with their sexuality. Childbearing will be the biological norm for the woman, the implications of which must necessarily invade her entire psycho-sexual function. The entire procreative process, from conception through lactation, deeply involves the woman in the nurturing of life, an intimate relatedness which can hardly be severed by cutting the umbilical cord.

Doris Lessing, quoted in *Harper's* magazine, July, 1973, says, "I know a lot of girls who don't want to get married or have children. And very vocal they are about it. Well, they're trying to cheat on their biology . . . . It will be interesting to see how they're thinking at thirty." It is significant to note that Doris Lessing is a frequent contributor to *Ms* magazine. It is difficult to deny that a woman's creativity is largely involved with relationships and with the nurturing of life symbolized and exemplified by the physical act of childbearing. When we soberly face the demands of motherhood, we may well be driven to despair or evasion, nonetheless the creative urge is undeniably there. God designed it not only for the perpetuation of the race but also for our human fulfillment as we demonstrate the motherhood of God in society.

To assure a fruitful and complementary relationship with the man, the woman is given desire for her husband. The character of that desire will determine the kind of rule exercised by her husband. We may as well acknowledge here that biblical and secular history both record the results of man motivated by woman, beginning with Adam, who responded to Eve's desire rather than to his own objective appraisal and his spiritual responsibility. Many battles have been fought over a woman whose lustful and self-centered desire has provoked a raging conflict among men to possess her. Much is being said today about women enslaved by men, with little outcry against predatory and designing females. Men may, on the whole, protest but feebly because, as a wise man once told me, men are not really deceived by this approach; they simply like the ego-trip. It is, however, a serious perversion of womanhood, and one which the Scriptures everywhere attempt to correct, with such words as "modesty," "decorum," "sensible," "seemly" (not seedy!), "serious," "temperate," "faithful," "well attested for good deeds," "devoted to doing good in every way," "chaste," and "reverent."

These are not negative words. They describe a godly woman, the woman who is the glory of man, the flower of humanity, who in turn motivates men to godliness, "without a word," as Peter says. The godly and mature woman's chief desire for a man is that he

should be godly and mature. I believe a woman motivates a man to godliness not so much by bringing him
to God as by *bringing God to him,* through a life that
consistently tells the story of God's giving, sacrificial
love. She motivates him to be a godly father by being
a godly mother. She motivates him to emotional sta-
bility and tranquillity by being peaceful in her inner
spirit, evidenced in gentleness and quietness. It is legitimate to desire him to be a good lover, as well, since
that is a part of his own fulfillment. And good lovers
are motivated by good lovers!

I am told that the Hebrew word for "rule" suggests
a possible retaliatory connotation. A woman whose
desire for her husband is centered in self-interest may
badger him into resigning his headship or becoming
tyrannical. A female letter writer in *Psychology Today*
suggests an alternate form of dominance: "It's better
to let them think they're king of the castle, lean and
depend on them, and continue to control and manipu-
late them as we always have." This kind of pseudo-
submission knows nothing of the dignity of servanthood, and is just as effective in defrauding a man as is a
more overt form of dominance.

> And to Adam he said, "Because you have
> listened to the voice of your wife, and have
> eaten of the tree of which I commanded you,
> 'You shall not eat of it,' cursed is the ground
> because of you; in toil you shall eat of it all
> the days of your life; thorns and thistles it
> shall bring forth to you; and you shall eat the
> plants of the field. In the sweat of your face

you shall eat bread till you return to the
ground, for out of it you were taken; you are
dust, and to dust you shall return" (Genesis
3:17–19).

A man's creativity is largely involved with his work.
I believe work is given to man as a therapy, and an
outlet for sexual energy. It is interesting that men who
think of themselves largely as "studs" are known as
"*play*boys." The way in which a man approaches his
work is critical to his development as a mature man.
Mr. Gilder, in July 1973, *Harper's* Magazine has
stated that a man is dependent upon woman to tie
him into the family unit. The Scriptures tell us how
she can do this: by giving him headship in the home!

A man who is the acknowledged head of his home
will not be inclined to make his work his mistress. He
will be motivated to provide for his family by means
of his work, but he will not need to use his work to
define his sexuality. If he has a home base in which his
emotional, physical, and spiritual needs are acknowledged and lovingly attended, then he will be free to
view his work as an outlet for his creativity. A home
which is in a state of upheaval and disorder will either
disorient him so that he cannot work or cause him to
take refuge in his work as an escape.

Again, a man is motivated in his view of work by
the woman's view of her work. The industrious, creative, secure woman of Proverbs 31 provides an at-
mosphere of strength and dignity. Her wisdom,
kindness and inner beauty provide emotional security

for her husband ("the heart of her husband trusts in her"). *The Living Bible* adds "and she will richly satisfy his needs." Her husband is thus freed for leadership: "he sits among the elders of the land."

There are thorns and thistles in everything we do. We work in a hostile environment. The perils of working in today's industrial society are certainly no less demanding than in an agrarian culture. The tensions and pressures symbolized as thorns and thistles are used as God's goads to maturity. Blessed is the man who finds an uncritical, sympathetic and alert listener in his home at the end of a day's toil. A woman who cares, who will pray with him through his stresses, is a balm in Gilead, a healing mercy.

It would be well for us to be aware of certain crisis periods through which both men and women pass, having to do with performance frustration. For the man, one of the most critical, psychologists say, is approximately age 40, give or take a few years. It is a kind of vista point from which he views the past and the future. The disparity between what is and what he had dreamed can be troubling. A woman's most unsettling time often coincides with major changes in the home structure, such as children leaving for college or marriage, or a geographical uprooting. Secular research can be valuable to an understanding of symptoms during these critical periods. However, we must know that these periods of stress graphically demonstrate the need to know who we are in terms of God's loving and wise purpose for our lives. Who we are rests upon who He is and not upon what we do.

Dorothy L. Sayers, quoted in *A Matter of Eternity,* writes:

> The Church's approach to an intelligent carpenter is usually confined to exhorting him not to be drunk and disorderly in his leisure hours, and to come to church on Sundays. What the Church *should* be telling him is this: that the very first demand his religion makes upon him is that he should make good tables. Church by all means, and decent forms of amusement, certainly—but what use is all that if in the very centre of his life and occupation he is insulting God with bad carpentry? No crooked table-legs or ill-fitting drawers ever, I dare swear, came out of the carpenter's shop at Nazareth.

True, we do not establish our identity through performance, but in the same way that "faith by itself, if it has no works, is dead" (James 2:17), so we evidence who we are by the diligent, orderly, creative function of our God-given abilities. If a choice must be made between financial affluence and work which suits the temperament, talents and spiritual gifts of either man or woman, then the truly godly choice will surely be to honor our humanity and live within the framework of who we are. In the beautiful words of Matthew 6:25–34, Jesus taught us to live with simplicity, an art for living which has been swallowed up in our materialistic society. In some families the man's only motivation to work is overspending or the mismanagement of household affairs, with the result that the man is so driven by financial indebtedness he is literally swallowed up by the necessity to provide materially for his family. Sometimes, then, the wife will also take a job, and the children are virtually orphaned, family communication breaks down, and spiritual goals are abandoned.

Your heavenly Father knows that you need to be fed and clothed, Jesus says, but anxiety concerning these needs belies our trust in Him and gives priority to the transient, temporal things, rather than to the eternal realities of the spirit. The Apostle Paul reminds us, in 1 Corinthians 7:28–35, that even the proper desire to please one another in marriage can be perverted with anxiety and preempt our primary reason for life: undivided devotion to the Lord. I believe we need to make periodic evaluation of the encroachment of worldly affairs in our lives. The work and worry syndrome, which never satisfies the insatiable demand for more and more things, fritters our God-given lives away on the nothingness of worldly status. In such a materialistic rat-race, we bear only "the image of the man of dust," by-passing the satisfaction and eternal glory of bearing "the image of the man of heaven" (1 Corinthians 15:45–50).

> The man called his wife's name Eve, because she was the mother of all living. And the Lord God made for Adam and for his wife garments of skins, and clothed them.
> Then the Lord God said, "Behold, the man has become like one of us, knowing good and evil; and now, lest he put forth

his hand and take also of the tree of life and eat, and live for ever"—therefore the Lord God sent him forth from the garden of Eden, to till the ground from which he was taken. He drove out the man; and at the east of the garden of Eden he placed the cherubim, and a flaming sword which turned every way, to guard the way to the tree of life (Genesis 3:20–24).

Until now, the woman is simply called Woman, translated from the Hebrew *Ishah,* which means "Out of Man." Now Adam changes her name to Chavah, which means Life. Eve is the English translation of Chavah. Adam may be affirming and assenting to Eve's believing response to God's promise of triumph over Satan and his seed by the seed of the woman, the Lord Jesus Christ, and all who through his atoning death and saving life are assured victory with him over the evil one. There will now be two divisions of humanity: those in Adam and those in Christ.

From the beginning the Lord God assured a nobility to womanhood, an intimate and sensitive role in his redemptive plan. All Scripture which is pertinent to the role of women will fit within this basic framework. The female mode is dedicated by God to a unique expression of redemptive life. There will be protective safeguards, as the Father-God guards the moral purity of his daughter, the symbolic bride of Christ.

With his questioning, God had led Adam and Eve

to confess "and I ate." "If we confess our sins, he is faithful and just, and will forgive our sins and cleanse us from all unrighteousness" (1 John 1:9). God then acted immediately to deal with their sin. The skins with which God clothed them necessitated the death of animals. This was God's preview of the way in which he would ultimately bear for us all the agony and cost of our rebellion, "the Lamb of God who takes away the sin of the world" (John 1:29).

Incidentally, Isaiah chapter 53, that exquisite passage predictive of our Lord's atoning death, contains a sensitive and highly suggestive imagery in verse 7.

> He was oppressed, and he was afflicted, yet he opened not his mouth; like a lamb that is led to the slaughter, and like a *ewe* that before *her* shearers is dumb, so he opened not his mouth.

I am told that the female sheep, or ewe, when faced with danger, has the ability to run, while the male sheep's legs "freeze" in similar circumstances. Thus, a ewe unresistant before her shearers would picture a *willing* submission, confirming what we have already seen in Philippians chapter two.

Adam and Eve were limited, finite creatures before their defiance of God, but they were perfectly contented and totally fulfilled, with no sense of inadequacy, frustration or failure. Their humanity was totally possessed by the life-giving love of their Father-God, and this state of perfect fulfillment is symbolized in their unashamed nakedness. Severed from their source of life and love and faced with their resultant inadequacy and guilt, they misappropriated one of God's own gifts to them to contrive a cover-up for their shame. Fig leaves, magnanimous and beautiful but lifeless apart from the tree, portray so well our efforts to live fruitful and fulfilled lives apart from God. Our best efforts are like roman candles on the fourth of July, a loud noise, a brief moment of glory and the inevitable fizzle.

God offers to replace our shabby human efforts with the impeccable righteousness of his Son, so that thus clothed we may be acceptable before God, free to enjoy the love relationship with him which assures our identity and sense of worth.

But the Pandora's box has been opened by their disobedience. God knows the self-imposed curse of self-centeredness with which they have been infected. Only God can judge good and evil by himself, for he is Good. When we make our self-interest the criterion for good, we have a formula for disaster. We have polluted our humanity and our whole environment with our self-centeredness. It would be unthinkable that we should live endlessly in this state! Anticipating this, God sent the man out of the garden of Eden and guarded that access to the tree of life. Significantly, he relates both the charge and the dismissal from the garden to the man, again acknowledging his governmental headship. In leaving with him, Eve acknowledged both God's authority and Adam's headship.

It is generally agreed that the cytoplasm of the ovum is not mortalized; that it is mortalized only in union with the sperm. At any rate, the Scriptures teach that humanity was infected by sin through Adam (Romans 5:12), but a new birth is possible by faith "not of perishable seed but of imperishable, through the living and abiding word of God" (2 Peter 1:23). Jesus Christ, born of woman, conceived by the Holy Spirit, is the Living Head of the new humanity. In him we possess life, abundant and eternal.

Submissive to our Living Head, we may experience the deep healing of our humanity. God will deal with the root-issues, our attitudes toward him, ourselves and others. Every encounter with another person is an encounter with Christ. The cup of cold water given in His name, or the bitter thrust of criticism or hostility. A simplistic fashioning of fig leaves stamped "I'm okay, you're okay," will be only a temporary expedient, a brief lull in the storm, if it does not issue from a heart conquered by God's love, forgiveness and acceptance.

The built-in tensions of life can be creative or destructive. The pain, the thorns and thistles, are the ever-present reminders of humanity's limitations, that "all we like sheep have gone astray; we have turned everyone to his own way." "Weeds are nature's way of filling a vacuum," a gardener told me. The remedy, he suggests, is a closely woven pattern of "good" plants.

Temperamental, cultural, racial, sexual differences between people are the stuff of which our daily lives consist. There is also the necessary authority structure: teacher-student, government-citizen, parent-child, husband-wife, etc. In it all there is what the Apostle Paul calls "the law of sin and death," and what science refers to as the law of entropy (i.e. inexorably increasing randomness or disorder). It is sheer realism to state that life is not fundamentally romantic, but basically tragic, and in constant need of redemption. Pessimism and despair say there are no answers, no solutions. Romantic idealism seeks the pot of gold at rainbow's end. Christian idealism is grounded in the integrity and character of God, a quality of life which he offers to us in a growing, maturing relationship of love and trust.

The quality of that life, described as "love, joy, peace, patience, kindness, goodness, faithfulness, gentleness, self-control" (Galatians 5:22,23) will invade the vacuum in our individual lives and in society, resolve tensions creatively, and reverse life's entropy by the redemptive power of the resurrection. The method to appropriating that kind of life is in knowing the One in whom it resides, the Lord Jesus Christ, knowing him as First Cause and First Love!

12. *Woman in the Law*

The acupuncture rationale sees disease as resulting from an unbalanced energy flow. This theory sees dual forces of "yin" and "yang" moving through twelve meridians. "Yin" is female and negative, while "yang" is male and positive. The acupuncturist carefully selects the points for his needles, then inserts them to stimulate a balanced flow of energy through "yin" and "yang." The "yin" (female) is front body, the "yang" (male) is back.

This information, related by a skilled acupuncturist, reminded me, among other things, that recorded in Exodus 33:23 the Lord said to Moses, " . . . you shall see my back; but my face shall not be seen." The context was the giving of the Law to the people of Israel. The back provides structure, strength, and support to the body, while the front provides its social function and expression. In the letter of the Law we see the moral structure of our humanity in the context of the strength and authority of God, the Father. In the living Word of God, the Lord Jesus Christ, we see "the image of the invisible God" (Colossians 1:15), "For in him the whole fulness of deity dwells bodily" (Colossians 2:9), and "he reflects the glory of God and bears the very stamp of his nature, upholding the universe by the word of power" (Hebrews 1:3). In the Person of the Lord Jesus Christ we have the full expression of the moral character of God—both authority and submission, Father–Mother, law and grace, prohibition and liberty. In him is the perfect harmony of male–female and, in fact, of masculinity–femininity. He is the full expression of the love of God "which binds everything together in perfect harmony" (Colossians 3:14). "He is both the first principle and the upholding principle of the whole scheme of creation" (Colossians 1:17, Phillips paraphrase). The Lord Jesus Christ is life's synthesis!

We are told that Moses had a face-to-face relationship with God, that God spoke to Moses "as a man speaks to his friend" (Exodus 33:11). The Gospel of John tells us (1:18) that "no one has ever seen God; the only Son, who is in the bosom of the Father, he has made him known." Hebrews 11:23–28 tells the story of Moses' faith in the promised Messiah, which sustained and motivated him through insurmountable difficulties which "he endured as seeing him who is invisible." Moses saw beyond the letter of the Law to the living reality of the Lord Jesus Christ who was to come, therefore, he had an intimate relationship with God.

There were godly women, as well, who envisioned a God-anointed Savior, the Messiah. As did Moses, these women looked beyond the letter of the Law to its fulfillment in Christ. Such were Anna the prophetess, Elizabeth the cousin of Mary, and Mary the mother of Jesus. "Now the man Moses was very meek, more than all the men that were on the face of the earth" (Numbers 12:3). Anna, Elizabeth, and Mary are pictured as gentle, devout women of great spiritual beauty. "Blessed are the poor in spirit, for theirs is the kingdom of heaven!"

These humble persons were in stark contrast with the religious leaders who disfigured their faces "that their fasting might be seen by men," who blew trumpets in the synagogues to announce their almsgiving. Unsubmissive to the Lawgiver, they used his Law to gain personal prestige, and, blinded by their own self-centered perspective, they crucified the Lord of glory whom the Law prefigured.

The Law was not given to redeem, but to reveal the need for redemption. Our failure to keep the law reveals our spiritual poverty, our yen for rebellion, and above all our self-centeredness. Law is a necessary containment of evil, but it is not the cure. The Law given by God to Moses contains three basic elements: (1) God's intent for our humanity, the moral framework within which we may image his character; (2) the stimulus to our sin nature, which produces either rebellion or humility; (3) the symbolic revelation of God's redemption to be consummated in the death and resurrection of the Lord Jesus Christ.

In the Law, as in all of Scripture, we have God's view of sexual distinctives. *A Law based on equality of worth.* The Law challenges our self-centeredness by asserting the prior claim of the Creator-God: Thou shalt have no other gods before me; the equal status of all humans; love thy neighbor as thyself; and the distinctives of sexual function based on our creative purpose of God's own people; imaging God's father-mother attributes and our voluntarily submitting to his loving authority. I hope to demonstrate that Jesus and the apostles viewed the Old Testament Scriptures from this perspective.

The effect of human reasoning divorced from the revelation of God's Spirit is alienation from truth. It is like boarding a ship without a rudder. God's Law, interpreted by human reasoning, led to the crucifixion of his Son. Our view of God determines our perspective on ourselves and others. There is, in fact, no rationale for human equality apart from the creature-to-Creator relationship. If we do not belong to God, then we must compete for worth and status. It is understandable, then, that much of the rabbinical teaching and tradition misapplied and misinterpreted the Divine intention of the Law as it relates to the male–female relationship.

However, it is Jesus himself who warns us that we must expect to be judged by the same criterion with which we judge others. Is the male chauvinism of which we accuse the discriminating rabbis any more distorting to truth than the defensiveness born of envy and self-pity? A hostile misuse of Scripture and lack of reverence for God and others is often evident in the feminist ranks (both non-Christian and Christian, sad to say). It seems to me it is one thing to establish right, another to fight for our rights.

With a light touch, but telling implications, *Christianity Today*'s Eutychus, March 16, 1973, twits our feminist method of Scripture interpretation. I quote in part.

> Too long we men have been silent about the sexist nature of the Bible. Without question an anti-masculine stance characterizes the Scriptures in general.
>
> It begins right at the beginning. Apparently Miriam and Zipporah got to Moses and muddled his mind. In Genesis 4:26 he comments about the third generation of the race that "at that time *men* began to call upon the name of the Lord." Moses apparently assumes that women either (a) did not need to call upon the name of the Lord or (b) were already doing so. The passage is an obvious, unforgivable slight to men.
>
> And who are the perverted in the city of Sodom? The men, of course (Genesis 19:4). Presumably the women had kept their virtue in the midst of all this masculine depravity.
>
> Moses' crowning insult to men is recorded in the first chapter of Numbers. When it was necessary to gird for war to take the promised

land, notice who was numbered to go. Right again—the men! Women were too valuable to expend in war.

And when the writer of Proverbs wants to describe wisdom to his son, does he picture a bearded sage with snowy locks? Surprise—wisdom is a she (Proverbs 1:20)!

Paul, often pictured by feminists as the original male chauvinist pig, is in actuality a detractor of men. He boldly asserts that in Adam all die (1 Corinthians 15:22). If you will check the data closely in Genesis 3, you will find that it was mother Eve who took the first forbidden nibble. Paul blithely sails over this evidence and fixes the blame on poor old Adam. Gentlemen, we've been had.

So there you have the whole unhappy business. It just goes to show that a little proof-texting and some phony exegesis will prove anything.*

Under God, male headship-responsibility is as supportive of woman as female submission is of man. God is no chauvinist!

In Exodus chapter 20 the neuter language gender is consistently used throughout. In only three cases is there any sexual differentiation. The first occurs in verse 5: "you shall not bow down to them or serve them; for I the Lord your God am a jealous God, visiting the iniquity of the *fathers* upon the children to the third and fourth generation of those who hate

*Copyright 1973 by *Christianity Today*. Used by permission.

me . . . ." Eutychus might ask, facetiously, ". . . and what about the iniquity of the mother?"

God has offered himself to his people as the I AM, the eternal God, the I-AM-all-you-need God. He has reminded them that anything or anyone to whom their worship is diverted is an idol—a shallow, superficial, and perilous imitation of the God Who Is Enough. It is God's creative intent that we should become godlike by worshiping him! The peril in worshiping what is not God is that in so doing we will become like what we worship. Idolatry is our attempt to get what we want out of life, and to get it apart from a relationship of love and obedience to God. Idolatry is simply self-worship, and God, jealous for us, on our behalf, knows that self-worship is self-destructive.

The prophetic pronouncement of Genesis 3:16 "yet your desire shall be for your husband, and he shall rule over you" assists our understanding of this passage. God is again addressing the headship-responsibility of the man in the individual family unit, and the extended influence of man as father in society. The man whose worship is pure and undiverted from God will be the first link in a chain of family and societal healing. His headship in the home will be characterized by a reverent dependence upon God for the awesome responsibility of providing for his family in every dimension. If in his headship the man demands worship which belongs only to God, or evidences self-worship by materialism, self-indulgence, tyranny or arrogance, he will initiate attitudes in his children which will metastasize through them into society.

How responsible, then, is the mother and/or wife
whose desires are a motivating influence, a catalyst
giving incentive, negative or positive, to the man!
Headship is God's way of assuring governmental responsibility in the family unit, and the extended
influence of the family in society. It does not establish
sovereign rights. They belong only to God. Neither
does it absolve others from accountability. The some-
what different functional perspective of mother and
father are just the complement needed to assure a
balanced and sensitive approach to parenthood.

Eutychus will surely raise a question about the sab-
bath day as delineated in Exodus 20:10:

> . . . but the seventh day is a sabbath to the
> Lord your God; in it you shall not do any
> work, you, or your son, or your daughter,
> your manservant, or your maidservant, or
> your cattle, or the sojourner who is within
> your gates . . . .

Looks like a field day for male chauvinism—everyone gets a vacation except mom! Apparently, however,
even the most astute rabbis failed to note the potential
in this passage. Or could it be that with genuine
reverence for the "one flesh" unity of marriage they
concluded this commandment was addressed to man
and woman equally.

One more commandment, the last, is addressed to the
male:

> You shall not covet your neighbor's house;
> you shall not covet your neighbor's wife, or
> his manservant, or his maidservant, or his ox,

or his ass, or anything that is your neighbor's (Exodus 20:17).

We will not be tempted to ask whether women are free to covet, aware of the sober words of the Apostle Paul in Colossians 3:5, "Put to death therefore what is earthly in you . . . and covetousness which is idolatry." Covetousness is the corruption of worship, and so we are again reminded that male headship-responsibility is authenticated by his worship of God alone.

I believe the fact that this commandment is addressed to the man is an acknowledgment of him as the aggressor and initiator. In this case, it is not only a safeguard to his worship, but a protection for woman. In view of the responsibility thus enjoined upon the man, the predatory woman is seen as indulging in foul play and, in fact, reversing sexual roles. The commandment forbidding adultery is addressed to both, as are all the commandments addressed to mankind's inhumanities toward one another. These grow out of self-centered desire. The antidote to that root of all evil is a God-centered perspective born of purity of worship. In this, man is to set the pace. This is to be the foundation, the basic premise of his headship-responsibility.

Similar sexual distinctives are seen in the Levitical procedure. With a few significant exceptions, male animals are required for sin and guilt offerings—again acknowledging male headship-responsibility. Exceptions are found in Exodus 4:27, where a female animal

is required "if any one of the common people sins,"
contrasted with sins of a ruler, and Numbers 15:27
and Leviticus 5:1–6 where a female animal is offered
for sins committed "unwittingly." Again, this simply
acknowledges the female symbolism for the complement to headship-responsibility. It cannot and does
not imply inferiority, but distinctiveness of function.

> If a man's offering is a sacrifice of peace
> offering, if he offers an animal from the herd,
> *male or female,* he shall offer it without
> blemish before the Lord (Leviticus 3:1).

Peace, it's wonderful! How many times I have
wished I could trace with the Apostle Paul the Old
Testament passages which led him to conclude, as he
does in Galatians 3:28: "There is neither Jew nor
Greek, there is neither slave nor free, there is neither
male nor female; for you are all one in Christ Jesus."
Surely this was one of the passages from which the
Spirit taught him that in Christ there are no "dividing
walls of hostility." Christ Jesus is our peace. In
Ephesians chapter 2, He himself [Christ] is our peace,
who made both groups into one. "If you are Christ's,"
he says, "then you are Abraham's offspring, heirs according to promise" (Galatians 3:29), and children
of the "free woman" (Galatians 4:31).

To quote C.H.M. on Leviticus: "The language of
the peace offering is, 'it is meet that *we* should make
merry and be glad,—Let *us* eat and be merry.'"
Through Christ Jesus we have peace with God, and
having peace with God we have fellowship and com-

munion with all the saints. There are no second-class citizens in the kingdom of heaven, nor in the Church of Jesus Christ. "For in Christ Jesus you are all *sons* of God" (Galatians 3:26), spiritually autonomous in identity, with mutual access to God, equal status as his children, and joint-heirs to every spiritual resource.

In the burnt offering, the levitical priests could dispense their responsibilities as representatives of a sinning people; they symbolized this responsibility in the offering of a male animal. In the peace offering they witness the pleasure of God with a people at peace with him through obedience and repentance. This is the shared fellowship and communion with the God of all flesh.

Another passage which appears demeaning is Leviticus 12:2, "If a woman conceives, and bears, a male child, then she shall be unclean seven days"; verse 4, "then she shall continue for thirty-three days in the blood of her purifying"; verse 5, "If she bears a female child, then she shall be unclean two weeks, as in her menstruation; and she shall continue in the blood of her purifying for sixty-six days."

An article in *Look* magazine, April 21, 1970, "How to Choose Your Baby's Sex" suggests a probable reason for the Levitical procedure. Dr. Shettles, a distinguished gynecologist, has made observations which indicate "the male is the weaker sex—even before conception." On the basis of his research, he offers procedures for sex-selection. I quote in part, first from the procedure for female offspring:

No abstinence from intercourse is necessary, until after the final intercourse two or three days before ovulation. A low sperm count increases the possibility of female offspring, so frequent intercourse, prior to the final try two or three days before ovulation, cannot hurt and may actually help.

And from the procedure for male offspring:

Prior abstinence is necessary: intercourse should be avoided completely from the beginning of the monthly cycle until the day of ovulation. This helps ensure maximum sperm count, a factor favoring androsperms.

It would appear that the Levitical procedure may be part of God's plan for keeping nature in balance.

Another passage which appears to be discriminatory against females is Leviticus 27:2–8:

When a man makes a special vow of persons to the Lord at your valuation, then shall your valuation of a male from twenty years old up to sixty years old shall be fifty shekels of silver, according to the shekel of the sanctuary. If the person is a female, your valuation shall be thirty shekels. If the person is from five years old up to twenty years your valuation shall be for a male twenty shekels and for a female ten shekels. If the person is from a month old up to five years old, your valuation shall be for a male five shekels of silver, and for a female your valuation shall be three shekels of silver. And if the person is sixty years old and upward, then your valuation for a male shall be fifteen shekels, and for a female ten shekels. And if a man is too poor to pay your valuation, then he shall bring the person before the priest, and the priest shall value him; *according to the ability of him who vowed* the priest shall value him.

Taxes, taxes! The Jewish community had them too. And if these tax evaluations appear demeaning, think how degrading it is for women and children to be considered tax exemptions! Obviously these tax evaluations were based on earning power, past, present, or future, and the male was expected to be the breadwinner.

The foregoing is, of course, a cursory examination of the Law as it relates to sexuality. I offer it simply as a positive mode of interpreting the intent of the God who made us for himself, in whose eyes male and female are equal in identity, but different in function. I believe it evident that both Jesus and the apostles so viewed the Old Testament Scriptures, and that the full-orbed humanity of woman is unthreatened from Genesis to Revelation. God's Law acknowledges our spiritual mutuality as well as our sexual distinctives, and in it we are given a system of control over our propensity to misuse our humanity as sexual beings. The Law itself is perfect, but it must be interpreted, motivated, implemented and fulfilled by the Spirit of God.

And what was the response of the people to the Law

given by God through Moses? "And all the people answered together and said, 'All that the Lord has spoken we will do' " (Exodus 19:8).

> So they came, both men and women; all who were of a willing heart . . . dedicating an offering of gold to the Lord.

God's revelation is, of course, always a consistent fabric of Truth. His creative intent for his people never varies. Since the infiltration of evil in Eden, God has been shoring up our rebellion, but always before the coming of our Redeemer there was the continuing promise of his advent, and the redemption which would follow. Those who anticipated his coming by faith offered up the levitical sacrifices as symbolic of the Messianic atonement. For others, it was simply a performance, a nod to God, a bid for social prestige, a salve to conscience—all the gestures common to contemporary religiosity.

To God's men, then as now, the Law was not a pedestal for the display of their power and self-righteousness. To God's woman, then as now, the Law was not a put-down, but a guardian of the precious gift of womanhood. Proverbs chapter 31, most eloquent of all descriptions of a woman of dignity, was written by Lemuel, king of Massa, taught to him by his mother! In the Old Testament women were given redemptive positions suitable to their gifts. Miriam, sister of Moses, is highly revered even in rabbinical tradition. Deborah was a capable judge. Two Old Testament books are named for Ruth and Esther, noble and godly women. Rahab, the redeemed harlot, joins Sarah, wife of Abraham, in the Hebrews chapter 11 hall of fame, and is listed in the genealogy of Jesus Christ!

But then, as now, the woman who tries to establish her own identity, to function as a slave to her own self-centered demands, demeans her womanhood and earns the ill-repute that breaks her heart and infects her society.

Teach us thy way, O Lord. Teach us thy way! And restore in us your image, through the Living Presence of the Lord Jesus Christ!

13. *Woman in the New Testament*

The angel Gabriel was sent from God to a city of Galilee named Nazareth, to a virgin . . . and the virgin's name was Mary . . . and said "Hail, O favored one, the Lord is with you! . . . Do not be afraid, Mary, for you have found favor with God . . . The Holy Spirit will come upon you, and the power of the Most High will overshadow you; therefore the child to be born will be called holy, the Son of God."

And Mary said, "My soul magnifies the Lord, and my spirit rejoices in God my Savior, for he has regarded the low estate of his handmaiden. For behold, henceforth all generations will call me blessed; for he who is mighty has done great things for me, and holy is his name . . . he has put down

the mighty from their thrones, and exalted
those of low degree . . . He has helped his
servant Israel . . . as he spoke to our fathers,
to Abraham and to his posterity for ever."
—Excerpts from Luke 1.

Surely the greatest honor bestowed upon any human
being was the dignity of bringing to birth God's own
Son. Yet in all the feminist literature I have surveyed,
not once have I seen a reference to this Scripture,
though many others have been quoted or misquoted.
We will note a few of the many ways in which it is
relevant to womanhood.

First, I believe we need to see God in action. God
intervening on behalf of his people, in his own way, in
his own time. God had chosen the nation Israel to
demonstrate to the world his ways with his people.
This nation was in trouble. Since 586 B.C. when Jerusalem fell to the Babylonians and the Temple was
destroyed, Israel had had no real independence. According to Josephus, no man's life and no woman's
honor was safe under Herod the Great. Within the
nation, the high priesthood became an object of bar-
gaining, the sacred office sometimes going to the high-
est bidder. Victor Buksbazen says in his book, *Miriam
the Virgin of Nazareth:*

> It was a tragic irony that the Hasmonean
> dynasty, which started out as a revolt against
> idolatry and foreign rule, in the end suc-
> cumbed to alien ways and culture.

In this context, the condition of women was less

than desirable. The priesthood, Israel's key to national health, had been infiltrated with pagan ideology and compromised worship. Adjunct to this was an unwholesome view of woman's worth. The very points in the law which were meant to secure to the woman spiritual headship and marital fidelity were twisted to imply women were inferior and were used to license polygamy or promiscuity for men. According to most rabbinic customs of Jesus' time women were not allowed to study the Torah. Eliezer, a first-century rabbi, stated: "Rather should the words of the Torah be burned than entrusted to a woman. . . . Whoever teaches his daughter the Torah is like one who teaches her lasciviousness." The Talmud states: "Let a curse come upon the man who (must needs have) his wife or children say grace for him." There was a three-fold thanksgiving in the daily prayers of Jews: "Praised be God that he has not created me a gentile; praised be God that he has not created me a woman; praised be God that he has not created me an ignorant man."

In the great temple at Jerusalem women were limited to one outer court which was five steps below the court for men. In the synagogues the women were separated from the men, and were not allowed to read aloud or take any leading function. A rabbi regarded it as beneath his dignity to speak to a woman in public. Women were not allowed to bear witness in a court of law.

We may assume that women, then as now, rebelled both outwardly and inwardly against such attitudes and treatment. For example, when one reads of women being permitted to lay their hands on the sacrificial animal, the following is added: "Not that that was customary for women, but was to appease the women." Rabbinic sayings about women, such as "they are greedy at their food, eager to gossip, lazy and jealous," indicate not only a deplorable attitude toward women, but a lack of self-respect among the women themselves.

But then, as now, God knew about Israel's plight and he cared about its vagrant men and hurting women. "When the time had fully come, God sent forth his Son, born of woman, born under the law, to redeem those who were under the law, so that we might receive adoption as sons" (Galatians 4:4,5). God, who knew and cared about the individual also had a world view. God so loved the world (and all individuals who comprise it) that he gave his first-born to be the spiritual Head of a new humanity in whom "There is neither Jew nor Greek, there is neither slave nor free, there is neither male nor female; for (we) are all one in Christ Jesus" (Galatians 3:28). The Lord Jesus Christ, born a male, indicating the authority of his deity, born of woman and therefore free of Adam's sin, born under the law that he might fulfill it perfectly in spirit and in truth, was God's solution to the human dilemma. He revealed that redemptive plan, not to the rebellious who fought for their rights, but to the godly who waited before him in humility and faith.

Note the quality of womanhood in Mary, mother of Jesus, whose betrothed husband, Joseph, so respected her that though the law required the death penalty for infidelity he "being a just man and unwilling to put her to shame, resolved to divorce her quietly" (Matthew 1:19). To that quality of manhood, God responded with the revelation of his plan for Jesus' birth. Similarly, note the godliness and mutual respect of Zechariah the priest and his wife Elizabeth who were "both righteous before God, walking in all the commandments and ordinances of the Lord blameless." While the custom was to divorce a wife who was childless, this man and woman had a spiritual unity which transcended the cultural practices and expectations. God honored their mutual trust with the birth of John the Baptist, though "Elizabeth was barren and both were advanced in years" (see Luke chapter 1). Luke chapter 2 also tells us of a godly man named Simeon, righteous and devout and "looking for the consolation of Israel," to whom the Holy Spirit revealed the birth of Jesus. And there was a prophetess, Anna, who "did not depart from the temple, worshiping with fasting and prayer night and day." Simeon and Anna were both brought by the Spirit of God to the Temple at the very hour when the child Jesus was brought there for the customary infant ritual, to witness the fulfillment of their Messianic hope and faith.

Characteristic of these godly men and women was the integrity of their worship, their commitment to God's way of deliverance, in which they evidenced their spiritual equality and mutual respect. Singularly absent from all was concern for personal rights, but all had invested their hopes and prayers in God's larger plan—the redemption of Israel and the Gentiles. Preoccupied with what God was doing to meet humanity's needs and willing to be expended to that end, they were met individually and united around the Person of His Son. It was their involvement with him which gave them dignity and honor before one another; they were willing to yield their personal autonomy to the larger framework of God's world. This is the perspective that frees us all from the up-tight, threatened preoccupation with our rights and status.

If we get our toes stepped on by the insensitive or unwitting, we may certainly say "ouch," but a retaliatory crusade violates every Christian ethic. We may safely leave our case with the One who when he was reviled, did not revile in return, but trusted in Him who judges justly. This is the Jesus of Nazareth who was so totally free of all the cultural prejudices of his time on earth that some contemporary writers refer to his "feminist attitude" toward women.

Luke 8:2, 3, and Mark 15 record that many women followed Jesus, some of whom are identified. The cultural pattern in which these women lived would have prohibited them from religious study, and in fact from leaving their households. Of Mary of Bethany the Gospel writers record a tender and costly act of devotion which the Lord memorialized in a lasting tribute to her spiritual insight. Mary Magdalene was permitted the honor of being the first person to see the resurrected Lord. She was then commissioned by him to bear witness to his resurrection to the disciples, although custom eliminated the witness of a woman.

Jesus Christ touched the lifeless body of Jairus's

daughter, and praised the faith of the ceremonially unclean woman who touched his garment (Matthew 9:20–22). In both cases, he was distinguishing between the spiritual symbolism and/or sanitary requirements of the law and the essential worth of the individual. He was teaching that the essential value of a person before God is not changed by his or her function. Contrary to rabbinical interpretation, God is not displeased with a woman who is menstruating; it was simply a function which needed to be acknowledged for purposes of sanitation. Also, symbolically, the flow of blood and a dead body would both be reminders of human finiteness.

Jesus initiated conversation with the Samaritan woman at the well of Jacob (John 4:7–42) and his disciples "marveled that he was talking with a woman." In this instance, also, he strengthened the testimony of a woman, and validated her as a redeemable person.

In the home of Mary and Martha, Mary was commended for taking what was considered a cultural male role, while Martha who was performing in the typical woman's function, was gently rebuked for having her priorities reversed. As with men, women must give first precedence to worship so that function does not become a distraction (Luke 10:38–42).

Luke also records an interesting incident in chapter 11, verses 27, 28.

> As he said this, a woman in the crowd raised her voice and said to him, "Blessed is the womb that bore you, and the breasts that you sucked!" But he said, "Blessed

131

rather are those who hear the word of God
and keep it!"

It is plain that it was not Mary's biological function
which gave her distinction, though by it she bore
Jesus himself, but rather her identification as a devout
and obedient woman of God. This identification gave
her status with God. And though the birth of the
Child gave dignity and meaning to the function of
childbirth (as the Apostle Paul may well mean in
1 Timothy 2:15), Mary's status as a person was considered neither inferior nor superior.

Jesus also strictly taught monogamous and lifelong
marriage, with the alternative of celibacy (Matt. 19:
3–12). Spiritual equality is not only signified by the
marriage relationship, but it is also the basis for its
uniqueness. It is to be an unbroken and unbreakable
relationship. Jesus reiterates this theme in Mark
10:6: "But from the beginning of creation, 'God made
them male and female. *For this reason* a man shall
leave his father and mother and be joined to his wife,
and the two shall become one.' So they are no longer
two but one. What therefore God has joined together,
let not man put asunder." Marriage is a symbol, for
the unity of male and female, the equality of both.

It is interesting to note, however, that although
Jesus' respect for women as totally human and equal
in identity with men is unquestionable, the twelve
apostles, whom he personally selected, were all men.
Certainly we are not going to accuse our Lord of cultural prejudice! It appears that none of the women

who followed him, deeply involved with his life and ministry from his birth to his death, ever clamored for equal rights with the apostles. The mother of the sons of Zebedee who requested positions of prominence for her sons in Jesus' kingdom, prompted Jesus to observe that he, "the Son of man came not to be served but to serve, and to give his life as a ransom for man," and "whoever would be great among you must be your servant, and whoever would be first among you must be your slave."

We are again reminded that maleness is the symbol of authority which ultimately has its source in the Sovereign Father-God. Male authority, in any dimension of life, is not a sign of superiority, but a complement to the female function of submission. Neither of these functional modes affects the essential identity of the person. All are "sons of God" (indicating our neutral sexuality in Christ), serving him and others in the context of our sexuality, telling *His* story, not ours!

There can be no conflict between Jesus' doctrine and Paul's. Paul simply took the principles taught by our Lord and, being inspired, applied them within his cultural context. From that premise, we will consider the major, and most contested, passages in the epistles concerning women.

There is, it seems to me, a striking similarity between Jesus' and Paul's relatedness with women. Paul followed the example of his Lord in encouraging and commending women to violate *cultural* tradition where cultural tradition violated the proper exercise of their spiritual gifts. Priscilla (or Prisca), wife of Aquila, in whose house the Roman Christians gathered, is greeted along with her husband as Paul's "fellow worker" (Romans 16:3). She also made tents, traveled, risked her neck and expounded the Way, with her husband and in the company of the Apostle Paul (Acts 18 and Romans 16). One could hardly think of Priscilla as a passive believer!

Phoebe, by whom the Apostle sent his letter to the believers in Rome, was a deacon of the church at Cenchreae. Paul asked for her a reception "as befits the saints," expressing his gratitude because "she has been a helper of many and of myself as well." Lydia was the first convert in Europe. She was a businesswoman, and a "worshiper of God." "And when she was baptized, with her household, she besought us, saying, 'If you have judged me to be faithful to the Lord, come to my house and stay.' And she prevailed upon us" (Acts 16:13–15). Her conversion resulted from an evangelistic thrust directed specifically to a women's prayer meeting! Note, she was a woman who could initiate response from men, but she did so with a proper appeal to their authority. "If you have judged me to be faithful to the Lord."

I believe this illustrates the subtle difference between male and female function indicated by Paul in 1 Corinthians 11:7–12:

> For a man ought not to cover his head, since he is the image and glory of God; but woman is the glory of man. (For man was not made from woman, but woman from

man. Neither was man created for woman, but woman for man.) That is why a woman ought to have a veil on her head, because of the angels. (Nevertheless, in the Lord woman is not independent of man nor man of woman; for as woman was made from man, so man is now born of woman. And all things are from God.)

Paul is dealing with the cultural view of veils as the symbol of authority of husband over wife. Paul is using a contemporary cultural pattern to affirm a spiritual principle. God's woman has the freedom to adapt to cultural modes, if they can be a vehicle for expressing truth (as in this case), or to defy cultural norms if they misrepresent her life in Christ (as in the case of immodest and suggestive apparel).

This passage is sometimes used to demonstrate an alleged prejudice of Paul against women; however, I cannot comprehend the basis for such interpretation. That woman is the glory of man is to me one of the most beautiful things that can be said about woman! Notice he does not say that she is the *image* and glory of man. She is the image of God, and that is why and how she may be the glory of man. Paul knows that it is our Godlikeness that makes us truly and wholly woman. It is in bearing his image that we find our identity and security. If Paul had said that we are to be the *image* and glory of man he would have been inconsistent with his affirmation of our spiritual equality in other passages. In this passage he is not dealing with our equality, our basic humanity, but with our

135

femaleness. To use the old philosophical argument about the chicken and the egg, when God states that the chicken comes first he does not therefore suggest that the egg loses status. The fact that the male was created first provides order but does not establish pre-eminence!

It is interesting that the Scriptures place the woman in the same relationship to man as the Son is to the Father. The Son is said to be the glory of the Father. Hebrews 3:1 tells us that Jesus Christ reflects the glory of God's image, and John tells us in his Gospel that in beholding Jesus Christ we behold the reflected glory of the Father. This helps us understand the importance of our function to humanity. If all believers are to reflect the glory of God through their relationship with the Lord Jesus Christ, it would seem, then, that the uniqueness of the male-female relationship can only be recognized in terms of subjection by the woman to the governmental responsibility of the man in marriage and in the church, the effects of which will profoundly affect all of society.

The Pauline view of marriage harmonizes perfectly with our Lord's view. Each partner in the prescribed monogamous, lifelong marriage is to yield to the conjugal rights of the other (1 Corinthians 7:1–5). They are to be subject to one another as fellow-believers, but "the husband is the head of the wife as Christ is the head of the church, his body, and is himself its savior. As the church is subject to Christ, so let wives also be subject in everything to their husbands" (Ephesians 5:21–24). According to God's order, man

136

is to set the pace spiritually, to direct the affairs of the home in such a way that God is worshiped and glorified (in this way man is the glory of God). His wife is to support and nourish that commitment (in this way she is the glory of man). A husband is to give himself up for his wife as Christ loved and gave himself for the church; he is to love her as his own body. *This is the reason for Christian marriage*: to demonstrate the mystery relationship between Christ and his bride, the church (Ephesians 5:25–33).

Far from being a suffocating relationship for either marriage partner, this design for Christian marriage frees each to be God's person, consistent with their sexual distinctives as well as their spiritual equality. The same pattern pertains to relationships within the church, where as brothers and sisters we respect one another's spiritual gifts and women are subject to the headship-responsibility of men in the function of those gifts. The man who properly understands his responsibility to nourish and cherish his wife's body as his own will relate with sensitivity to the women's spiritual function within the body of Christ. Culturally, an unmarried Jewish woman was under reproach, an unmarried Greek woman was a suspected profligate. Paul encourages women not to marry, that they may be "anxious about the affairs of the Lord, how to be holy in body and spirit" (1 Corinthians 7:34). Godly men in the church are to provide ministry opportunities for these women appropriate to their spiritual gifts and commitment.

1 Corinthians 11:5 says "any woman who prays or

prophesies with her head unveiled dishonors her head" and thus establishes that women are not prohibited entirely from speaking in church. The prohibitive passages pertain to (1) speaking in tongues (1 Corinthians 14:20–40), (2) speaking out during teaching times (1 Timothy 2:11, 12), and (3) teaching in such a way as to usurp the authority of the men (1 Timothy 2:12). Therefore, one can scarcely imagine a woman in a long-term teaching ministry over a congregation. This would almost inevitably put her in a position of headship-responsibility, which is clearly prohibited by these passages.

It seems evident that the purpose of Paul's statement of restraint upon women was to preserve and encourage male spiritual headship, in the home and in the church, and to maintain order in the church to facilitate the teaching of the Scriptures to both men and women. It is surely not his intention to muzzle spiritual gifts in either sex.

I believe today's church needs to be confronted with a challenge to use creatively the spiritual gifts invested in women. In many churches the only task to which women are considered suited is kitchen work and ministering to small children. Perhaps this is due to the false reasoning that men are unsuited for such ministries. It may be that we need to shuffle some "roles" and thus discover new aptitudes in both men and women! Acts 6:1–6 records that the task of serving tables was assigned to "seven men of good repute," who were commissioned for this work by prayer and the laying on of hands. This suggests both the possibility of men serving in this capacity and the dignity of this kind of ministry. There are no small chores in the church of Jesus Christ. Men who are free to share such chores in the home will be less inhibited about serving in these capacities in the church.

However, at no time, in any era, will it be either appropriate or effective for Christian women to clamor for their rights. Such an attitude is, in fact, evidence that we are not qualified for ministry. Throughout the New Testament, the mature and godly woman is characterized by a gentle and quiet spirit (note: not gentleness and quietness, as this may be an affectation, but a quality of spirit) which forms the basic and motivating thrust of her life. Further, all Christians are enjoined to consider their own vulnerability to temptation (Galatians 6:1) in restoring a fellow Christian overtaken in any trespass. The restoration is to be done in a spirit of gentleness. How ironic it would be for women to become dominant in church affairs through demanding the right to exercise their spiritual gifts!

It may well be that a wider use of Spirit-directed female subjectivity in the application of church doctrine might have alerted the church to a more sensitive relational approach and averted the rise of existentialism. We must learn from this and other reactionary movements, such as Women's Liberation, and then we must prayerfully guard against overcorrecting our own errors.

Another aspect of womanhood persistently dealt with by the Scriptures is female seductiveness. Older women, who have learned to be reverent in behavior, not to be slanderers or slaves to drink, are to teach what is good and to train the young women to love their husbands and children, to be sensible, chaste, domestic, kind, and submissive to their husbands. This is to insure that the word of God may not be discredited (Titus 2:3–5).

Modesty and decorum in dress and behavior are prescribed by the apostles. In contrast, designer Leo Narducci says that the woman who wears his revealing styles is one who is "sure of herself, who thinks of sex more openly . . . she's not concerned about nudity. She has a body and she knows it" (quoted in *Eternity* magazine, June, 1970). And to further quote Kerry Elliot in the article entitled "What the Well-dressed Woman Isn't Wearing."

> "Oh dear," you say, adjusting your straps to make yourself suddenly shapelier, "but I don't think of sex appeal when I wear my shorts and halter." Maybe you don't. But the fellows do. And I don't mean just the dirty old men either, unless you put most of the male population from puberty to senility in that category. If you don't believe me, read your ladies' magazines. The fashion writers know the words to use: "naughty, daring, seductive, slightly wicked . . . ."

To put it more positively, woman might be considered a part of God's art form, the outer beauty simply giving witness to an inner spirit made beautiful by surrender to the Lordship of Jesus Christ. Thus physical characteristics become of less importance to a man surrendered to his lordship. The woman who radiates the glory of his character is precious in God's sight and motivated to use her body as a means of communicating who God is to the world. Viewing our bodies as temples of the Holy Spirit will encourage cleanliness, order, creativity, and honest beauty. Christian beauty is *pure* art form.

The New Testament closes with a significant passage using woman as a symbol:

> And I saw the holy city, new Jerusalem, coming down out of heaven from God, prepared as a bride adorned for her husband . . . . the Bride, the wife of the Lamb . . . . the holy city Jerusalem coming down out of heaven from God, having the glory of God, its radiance like a most rare jewel like a jasper, clear as crystal. (Excerpts from Revelation 21.)

Consistently throughout Scripture, woman is used to symbolize the people of God—in the Old Testament she is Israel, in the New she is the church, the Bride of Christ. She is the glory of man and the flower of humanity as God intended it to be. What a contrast to our shallow fantasies, our shabby romanticism, our female manipulating. It is the contrast between a life dedicated to self-centeredness and a life committed to the glory of God.

> Truly, truly, I say to you, unless a grain of wheat falls into the earth and dies, it

remains alone; but if it dies, it bears much fruit. He who loves his life loses it, and he who hates his life in this world will keep it for eternal life (John 12:24, 25).

Like the leper who was declared ceremonially unclean, to "dwell alone in a habitation outside the camp" (Leviticus 13:46) our self-centeredness alienates us from God and man. Let us follow our Lord to the death of our self-centered demands, and rise with Him to abundant life. Because HE lives, we shall live also!

14. *The Parable of Motherhood*

The earth as Mother, the womb from which all living things are born and to which all return at death, was perhaps the earliest representation of the divine in protohistoric religions. The Great Mother Goddess, a more powerful incarnation of the female principle as life-force, reigned over the sky, earth and underworld and revealed herself to humankind in the ever-renewing productivity of the earth and the ever-recurring rhythms of the moon . . . And woman, who shared the prodigious magic of procreation and nurture, whose menstrual cycle mysteriously coincided with the lunar cycle was the terrestrial link in this cosmis orbit of fertility.

Fertility statuettes . . . tell us that for our Paleolithic ancestors the generative force of the universe focuses in the female body . . .

It is remarkable how many legends survive among preliterate cultures of an earlier matriarchal period and a violence uprising by men in which they usurped female authority.

According to "A myth . . . in the beginning the sorceress moon woman, Kra, taught women to dominate men through terror, transforming themselves into spirits by the use of masks. But the sun man, Kran, learned the secret and revealed it to the men. They promptly killed the women, sparing only the girls, and to legitimize their seizure of power they took over the masks and the magic." [1]

Mythology is a spurious historical record; nevertheless, it is an illuminating one. In it we may see the projected distortions of human thinking, our fantasies, delusions and illusions about ourselves and others. In it we see the struggle for dominance as it actually exists in human hearts. How ironic to align ourselves in opposition to others, male or female, only to find that in the process we are destroying ourselves as well!

We return to the words of Genesis 3:20:

The man called his wife's name Eve,
because she was the mother of all living.

It is understandable that pagan philosophers have misapplied and misinterpreted this Divine edict. One

[1] From "The Downfall of Woman," by Dena Justin, *Intellectual Digest*, October 1973, reprinted from *Natural History*.

wonders, however, how such a man as Thomas Aquinas should derive from it that woman is "a misbegotten female . . . made in the image of man, not God." Others, some Christian women included, have found these words, as well as some of the Apostle Paul's, threatening and demeaning. These individuals are reacting defensively to the misconceptions, rather than looking for God's loving intent.

Simone de Beauvoir, the eminent French feminist, says:

> It is in maternity that woman fulfills her physiological destiny; it is her natural "calling," since her whole organic structure is adapted for the perpetuation of the species. But we have seen already that human society is never abandoned wholly to nature. And for about a century the reproductive function in particular has no longer been at the mercy solely of biological chance; it has come under the voluntary control of human beings.

She then refers briefly to the use of contraceptives, from which is launched a plea for legalized abortion. It is not my intention to attempt a critique of Ms. de Beauvoir. However, she raises some issues which cannot be ignored since they are realities with which we must live and reckon. It is heartening to find this articulate feminist acknowledging that maternity is woman's physical calling. Granting this innate sense of physiological destiny, one can scarcely avoid the conclusion that abortion is a serious assault on the female psyche, quite apart from any religious connotations of guilt. A deep sense of frustration and even worthlessness is the common experience of many childless women as well. Much of the argument for legalized abortion seems to equate it with the surgical removal of a malignancy. It seems to me that quite apart from the religious and societal factors, nature demands a more sensitive evaluation.

In the one paragraph quoted, Ms. de Beauvoir raises two issues which are at once separate yet inextricable: the woman as an individual, and woman woven into the fabric of society. For while it is true that each of us must be autonomous in some sense, it is also true that "no man (or woman) is an island." Society is us! A deteriorating, sick society is made up of deteriorating and sick individuals. Our legal system is a vital factor in containing the brutality of one human against another, but the analgesic to pain will not cure its malignant cause. We must be prepared to face the consequences of the misuse of our sexuality, individually and corporately.

The function of the church has always been to direct compassion toward the symptoms of evil, and redemption to the cause. The true church of Jesus Christ is not an organization, but an organism comprised not of antiseptic superhumans, but redeemed sinners in varying stages of Christian maturity. The greatest hypocrisy of the church is not our political ambivalence, but the credibility gap between our verbal witness to truth and lives which deny it. The corrective to society's ills must be found in honest, pure, sensitive and loving sexual relationships within the community of Christ's disciples. Since we are God's ordained witness to truth, we must face the sexual inequities and ignorance within the community of believers with repentance and a relentless commitment to seeking and enacting God's truth with love.

My generation has inherited and perpetuated error, which, judging from much of the current literature, has provoked a reactionary response. The reactionary response in turn, will be overcorrected by their progeny. Truth out of balance becomes error! Let us pray for clear heads, and emotions controlled by a Spirit-directed focus on God's Word. Such a focus always faces life realistically. Only the Spirit of Truth can chart our course through the mish-mash of fantasy, illusion and intellectual speculation which comprises "natural" wisdom.

> And the Lord God made for Adam and for his wife garments of skins, and clothed them (Genesis 3:21).

This beautiful picture of God ministering redemption to his creatures remains the only solution to the human dilemma. The way out is the way back to the God who made us for himself, the God who made woman so that he could "mother" mankind through her.

Eve, we are told in Genesis 3:20, was so named "because she was the mother of all living." It seems apparent from the biblical account that only Adam and Eve and the animals were then living. Her name was prophetic, of course, because she would bear physical children. However, it seems evident that her motherhood was far more extensive and of deeper significance than the merely physical. I am convinced that the physical, sensory life is a parable of the spiritual. Eve was mankind's mother, equipped for her function by a special sensitivity toward life in all forms. Her physical anatomy symbolizes that she was equipped to nurture life, not as a mere "baby machine" but in every dimension: physical, emotional and spiritual.

Few would claim that human life exists in only a physical dimension. Most will acknowledge that humans are three-dimensional. The Apostle Paul acknowledges the whole person as spirit, soul, and body (1 Thessalonians 5:23). Surely the all-wise God who created us in his own likeness and image and designed us male and female would not fail to coordinate the functions of our humanity into an integrated unit. Since there are evident complementary physical differences between the sexes, there must also be a complement of emotional differences as well, spiritual equality serving as the basic human identity out of which the emotions and body function. Our sexuality, then, must encompass the whole person, and being a woman is a distinctive way of expressing our humanity, equal in value but different in mode from maleness.

The implications of Eve's name, together with the evident physical characteristics of the female, added to the cultural pattern most frequently acknowledged by society, indicate that the female mode is primarily one of nurturer. In the fourteenth century, Lady Julian wrote *The Sixteen Revelations of Divine Love.* The following is taken from this work. "God Almighty is our kindly Father; God All-Wisdom is our kindly Mother." Quoted in *Time* magazine, film critic Sandra Chevey says, "The consistencies of a patriarchal society are science, reason, and law, and in a matriarchal society they are art, magic, spirituality, and mystery." Dr. John Wakefield, a gifted industrial psychiatrist, has related the observation that a female executive who functions as a mother can maintain harmonious relationships and excel as an executive, because in the sensitivity of the female mode of nurturing she does not compete with men nor intimidate other women. A male executive, he continues, functions best as a father. If either attempts to reverse these sexual distinctives, relationships suffer and their executive function is jeopardized. Here again we see evidence that the mother-father functions are more than biological.

It is God's intention that every woman should function as a mother in society—as a spiritual mother, of which physical motherhood is symbolic. An interesting corroboration of this is found in John 19:25–27. The Lord Jesus spoke to his mother from the cross: "Woman, behold your son," indicating John the disciple. Then, to John: "Behold your mother." John was of course not Mary's son, but the Lord, addressing her as "Woman" to acknowledge her full-orbed womanhood, then assigned her to John as his spiritual mother.

Jesus, the master teacher, frequently taught through parables. Nature is replete with parables of spiritual truth. Our plastic, urbanized society has deprived us of rich lessons from soil, plant and animal life and a general relatedness to the world of nature. One such parable, however, surrounds us persistently: the parable of natural birth. From the beginning, God gave us this living stereograph diagramming the method for nurturing life in every dimension.

Someone has said that "soul sex" (meaning sex enacted in the context of spiritual unity) is the "ultimate trip" of humanity. Actually, it is but symbolic of our "ultimate trip," which is our relationship with the Lord Jesus Christ, without which the symbol would be empty and irrelevant. The act of sex is a *function* of our identity; it is not our identity. Motherhood is also a function, expressive of life in its three dimensions. Each may be seen in the three stages of physical pregnancy: inception, gestation, delivery.

Genesis 4:1 records in three small words the first conception in human history: "Adam *knew* Eve." The word, "knew," suggests that life is produced, results from, intimate relationship. A relationship in which those involved really understand one another. This approach would restore sanity, meaning, and fulfillment to human sexuality. Life is intended to emanate from love relationships.

Natural birth is initiated by intimate relationships. The matter of "knowing" one another implicates body, soul, and spirit.

> True sexuality is a function of the total personality, and is experienced and expressed only in the lives of genuinely mature people.
> Anybody listening carefully understands

that many people use sex as a language through which they whisper reassurance to themselves. That is the meaning of it for women or men who are uneasy about their own sexual identification and who use it to assure themselves of their femininity or masculinity rather than to communicate something to another person. It is perhaps the most tragic of all the uses of sex, because it leaves the man or woman fundamentally in isolation from another individual. This "reassuring" use only underscores our human capacity to make other people into means of achieving our own ends. Such an attitude is the death of any genuine reaching out to another.

These wise words are quoted from an article in *Redbook* magazine, May, 1972, "The Sex Mystique," by Father Eugene C. Kennedy. We cannot really know one another without communicating as whole persons. God communicates his life to us in all three dimensions; we are to communicate the beauty of his character in every area of our lives.

We can have "knowing" relationships, when we learn to receive others as living, redeemable human beings—not as inferiors, and therefore "projects," nor as superiors and therefore "objects" of worship. This is the principle of *receptivity*. The next step in the nurturing process is that of *response*, or relatedness. Once the life is initiated/received, then the whole body of the woman responds to that life within her, her entire metabolism matches the demands of that life. Followed by this is delivery, or the *release* of that life. Pregnancy terminates, the umbilical cord must be severed. This is a natural process with emotional and spiritual connotations.

The same pattern is followed in the new birth, or spiritual regeneration. We receive life; we do not initiate it. Spiritual life also emanates from relationship. "I know my sheep, and am known of mine," Jesus says (John 10:14). We cannot have spiritual life without that mutual, intimate knowing. Christ in me, and I in Christ, is not a casual relationship, a mere profession, a polite gesture, but a genuine possession of one another. God initiated our spiritual rebirth in the giving of his Son; it is up to us to receive him.

J. B. Phillips, in paraphrasing John 1:11, captures so well its poignancy: "He came to his own home and his own people received him not!" Natural and spiritual life are both contingent upon our willingness to be receivers. John 1:12 says, ". . . but to all who received him (the Lord Jesus Christ) he gave power to become children of God." We are spiritually reborn when we receive the life introduced by the Spirit of God, symbolized by the inception of physical life.

Our Lord said, "It is more blessed to give than to receive." But giving is the end of the process. Receiving is the means by which we learn to give; indeed, we have nothing to give until we have first received. Ephesians 3:19 says, " . . . and to know the love of Christ which surpasses knowledge, that you may be filled with all the fullness of God." Fullness of life results from intimately knowing Jesus Christ, whom we have received by faith.

The Apostle Paul beautifully expresses this again in Philippians 3:10, ". . . that I may *know him* and the power of his resurrection, and may *share his sufferings, becoming like him* in his death, that if possible I may attain the resurrection from the dead." This is the way in which God's image is restored in us. The more we know him and understand his ways, the more demonstrable our likeness to him. This intimate relatedness with Christ results in true self-realization. In this reciprocal knowing, we truly learn to know ourselves. Being identified with Jesus Christ means to live responsively to his life within us, to express the uniqueness of our individuality within the context of his character. We nurture God's life within us in the same way the mother's body responds to the growing fetus. We feed that new life with the milk and the meat of the Word of God. And as we submit to the demands of Christ's life within, our identification with him grows until we are able to say with the Apostle Paul, "I have been crucified with Christ; it is no longer I who live, but Christ who lives in me, and the life I now live in the flesh I live by faith in the Son of God who loved me and gave himself for me" (Galatians 2:20).

"But we have this treasure in earthen vessels, to show that the transcendent power belongs to God and not to us" (2 Corinthians 4:7). Then, as in the natural life where the fetus becomes the focal interest, the new taking precedence over the old, so, "though our outer nature is wasting away, our inner nature is being renewed every day." As the mother's body is intent upon giving over all the nutriments necessary to the development of that new life within, so all we have and are is to be given over to the development and expression of the indwelling life of Jesus Christ.

Release is the third stage. There is a beautiful freedom in the Christian life, a freedom to be our true selves. But it comes from being subject to the lordship of Jesus Christ. This is the continuing paradox of the Christian life. We are released from the bondage of the old law of sin and death to the new principle of life and resurrection. We are liberated from the agonizing bondage of the old life, "I do not do what I want, but I do the very thing I hate . . ." to a totally new principle, the law of the Spirit of life in Christ Jesus, that sets us free from the law of sin and death. (Contrast Romans chapters 7 and 8.) In the physical sense we may have sterility, abortive pregnancy or the full development and release to a new life dependency. There is sterility if we do not receive life, abortion if we do not nurture it, abundant life if we release it.

It is so also in the spiritual life. We have spiritual sterility (experienced emotionally and physically) if we do not receive Christ, aborted maturity if we do not nurture the new life with his Word and submit our will in obedience to him, and abundant life when we release his life to others, reproducing the character of Christ and making him incarnate for others to see and know. Released from the old self-centeredness, to the new liberty of dependency on Christ's life, we may teach and nurture that freedom in others.

The life of Jesus Christ which we receive by faith is meant to be disseminated into society in terms of his character. In receiving him we are reborn to a totally new resource for living: the love of God which serves and gives, forgives and accepts, for the sheer joy of loving. That quality of life is nurtured in us by knowing and communing with the Lord Jesus Christ, allowing his written Word to instruct us and his living Person to possess us. That relationship with him is consummated in fruitful relationships with others.

Romans 15:7 tells us how to begin: "So open your hearts to one another, as Christ has opened his heart to you, and God will be glorified" (Phillips paraphrase). Limitlessly Christ receives us; we can measure our receptivity to him by our openness toward others.

Christ received us when we had nothing to offer but hostility and death. So, too, we must learn to receive others where they are. Some have never experienced the new birth, but their physical, natural life is God's gift and we must be respectful of God's investment in every person. We must identify with other's needs as he identifies with ours, meeting us where we are, gently drawing us to himself.

In order to nurture life in others we must be willing to learn to know them. This cannot be rushed. It requires a willingness to be imposed upon and a commitment to listening. And a willingness to be candid about our own lives. I wonder if the well-known "woman's intuition" may not be at least partially due to a more highly developed faculty for listening than is commonly found in men. We must learn to know one another according to God's wisdom, evaluating our needs and desires by his standards, so that we may nurture his life and character in one another. This is "body life" relatedness, growing together through mutual response to God's will and purpose for our lives.

This quality of relatedness must begin with our most intimate relationships if it is to have relevance elsewhere. We cannot live double lives, showing one face at home and another in public. Spiritual motherhood, the nurturing of Christ's life in ourselves and others, is a total life-style. It is the outward function of our identity, the evidence that we are God's woman.

We are all surrounded by needy, hurting people. Recognizing these needs and responding lovingly to them is what life is all about. If we are living from day to day just grudgingly doing the necessary elementary things without exposing ourselves to involvement with others' needs, then we have not even begun to really live! We are aborting life, rather than nurturing it. God intends for us to project his life into the human stream. This we do in very practical ways, finding where people are hurting, establishing the level of need in our homes, our neighborhoods, the church community, or wherever our lives touch others. All too often we know others only in terms of how they relate to us, whether they suit us temperamentally or satisfy the demands we make of them. There may be strangers in our own homes, maybe even in our own beds.

In ministering to others, both they and we must be aware that as spiritual mothers we are only channels of life, not Life itself. We are only qualified to nurture life in others when we, as the Macedonians, have first given ourselves to the Lord and then to others (2 Corinthians 8:5). The recognition that we must continually draw upon him will prevent inordinate and unwarranted dependencies on us. We will then faithfully direct others to Jesus Christ as the source of life and encourage full dependency on him. We and all to whom we minister must learn to feed on the bread of heaven. When we develop dependencies on individuals, rather than on Christ, we are developing spiritual invalidism, simply dispensing emotional crutches.

True spiritual motherhood is described in Galatians 4:19: "My little children, with whom I am again in travail until *Christ* be formed in you!" We who have mothered physical progeny are often guilty of trying to reproduce ourselves in our children—our tastes, our culture, our frustrated ambitions—our image rather than God's. This can be extended to other relationships as well. Thus it is important that we do not use ourselves as the criterion for what is right and good, rather Christ.

Responding to other lives and nurturing Christ's life in them is often at least as painful as the process of natural birth. We cannot love without being vulnerable. However, while it hurts to love, the sterility of lovelessness is still more painful. The hurt we experience in order that Jesus Christ may be made known is the way in which we identify with his death, and that kind of identification is always followed by resurrec-

157

tion. It fulfills our humanity, gives significance and beauty to woman as nurturer and obeys our Lord's directive to be salt and light in the world.

Love is best experienced against a background of hostility; joy is greatest in contrast with sorrow; peace is at the core of the tornado. The quality of Christ's life transcends life circumstances. The expressions of his life are best displayed against the negative situations of our lives. Fully exposed, we may experience the full dimensions of genuine life.

"I have loved you with an everlasting love; therefore I have continued my faithfulness to you" (Jeremiah 31:3). In the Hebrew text the word "love" in this verse is in the feminine form. G. Campbell Morgan says, "This is another of the great texts in which that supreme and too often forgotten fact of the Motherhood of God gleams out through the sacred declaration, 'I have loved thee with an everlasting Mother-love.' "

Mother-love is here characterized as everlasting and faithful—but again, this is GOD'S love! Human love is conditional and profligate. But God offers to love through us; it is "Christ in you, the hope of glory." Weak human gestures at alleviating distress are merely a projection of our need to be needed. Providing emotional crutches, symptomatic salves, amplifying self-pity by coddling and pampering, is not nurturing the character of Christ. This is our human misconception of mother-love. Speaking the *truth* in *love* is God's way of building and nurturing us, and this is the method we are to use with ourselves and with others.

The godly woman ministers to others, not for ego-satisfaction (either her own or theirs) but that God may be glorified in his creation. This is her life-style and her life's goal. In the process of nurturing, we learn authentic tenderness, compassion and sensitivity. And what we have learned and demonstrated will become an example to others. Subject to our Father's authority, we may be mothers in society, whether or not we have produced physical progeny.

We return to the parable of birth, and what we have termed the principle of release. When a woman delivers a child, a new and different kind of relatedness develops. As we release, or express, Christ's life to others, we experience him in new ways. We see him through their eyes, their experiences of joy and sorrow. In loving others we are loving him; the cup of cold water dispensed in his name is given to him. Bearing fruit in every good work, we increase in the knowledge of God.

Spiritual motherhood is the expression of the femininity of God's character as seen in the servanthood of the Lord Jesus Christ. It is a dimension of maturity intended for every Christian, whatever our function.

Paul reminds the believers in Thessalonica in his first letter, chapter 2 verse 7 that "we were gentle among you, like a nurse taking care of her children." The word "nurse" translated from the Greek *trophos* is best translated "nursing mother." Paul also related to these believers as a father, described in verse eleven, "for you know how, like a father with his children, we exhorted each one of you and encouraged you and charged you . . . ." Here we see the demonstrated maturity of one whose expressed goal for himself and others is to "lead a life worthy of God, who calls you into his own kingdom and glory."

Paul is free to demonstrate the perfectly integrated character of the Lord Jesus Christ in whom all the fullness of the godhead is expressed bodily. Paul, whose natural temperament was aggressive to the point of violence, exhibits in his mature Christian manhood the gentle strength of his Lord. But though he was a spiritual father-mother, one could never think of Paul as an effeminate man. He faithfully assumed his male leadership-responsibility in which he manifested the fruit of the Spirit, which is the character of the Lord Jesus Christ (Galatians 5:22, 23).

Deborah, Israel's beloved prophetess and judge, led the nation as a "mother in Israel" (see Judges 5:7). Although God gave her a unique position of counselor to the nation, she used her God-given insight to support and encourage sagging male leadership-responsibility. In the account related in Judges chapter 4, she maintains a position of wise and supportive counsel while at the same time recognizing the command of the Lord to Barak to assume his leadership-responsibility (see verses 6 and 7). Deborah, wife of Lappidoth, prophetess, judge, was careful to preserve the delicate male-female roles even in an irregular situation. She preserved her sexual distinctive even in a position of counselor to a timid and insecure man.

Receiving others as lives whom God has given, to whom we may respond with adaptation and availability, is the way God intends all humans should live together. God intends us all, male and female, to share mutually all of the character-attributes of his Son, by the power of his Spirit, and in the exercise of his spiritual gifts. It is his intention that the distinctives of the male-female functions of loving authority and responsive submission be clearly recognizable in our function. Our identity as whole, integrated people in the Lord Jesus Christ, gives us the freedom to function as male or female, so the world may see demonstrated in our sexuality the love relationship between God who loves them and his people who are his love-slaves.

Like Mary, we may, subject to God's Spirit, make Jesus Christ incarnate. By her example, a woman may teach family, church and society the beauty and dignity of serving, nurturing and loving in order that the Lord Jesus Christ may live in us and among us. When we learn to live in this dimension, we will no longer be silent in the church or in society, but a living, vibrant mother to humanity's needs.

Then it may be said of us: "You've come a long way, baby!"

A Letter
Addressed to Men

You are much too busy to read a book, or you may have attempted to read this one and were baffled or bored. Will you accept a short letter?

You are no doubt familiar with Freud's famous quotation: "What does woman want? Dear God! What does she want?" Perhaps as a man you thought Freud was quoting you! Having been a woman for approximately a half century, having counseled and observed them in droves, having read widely from a mountain of literature—intelligent and inane, contemporary and ancient—I offer my studied and candid appraisal for your consideration. Most of the closeted and much of the public male discussion of women is directed toward the packaging. Perhaps you would consider a brief look at the content.

What does a woman want? The answer to that question depends upon what she thinks of herself. Women are human, just as men are. Thus, the two categories, superhuman (God and Satan) and extra-human (the world of things and nature), do not apply. Women are human, they relate to the other-than-human world in the same way you do. They deny or affirm the existence of God and Satan in word and/or in practice, and as a consequence, either rule or are ruled by things and nature.

If they deny God and affirm Satan, they are a god to themselves and life becomes a ego-centered bondage. Committed to self-pleasing, woman will use one of two modes to accomplish that end: she will be either "pussycat" (covertly aggressive) or "tiger" (openly aggressive). To further confuse you, she may use them alternately—one day (or moment) tiger, the next pussycat. Charming, isn't it? Popularly referred to as "the feminine mystique," it is an age-old technique, both tantalizing and terrorizing to the male. There are no rules for the game. The system of ethics which generally applies in other areas is superseded, and pretense, dishonesty, fraudulent use of bodies and minds, manipulative strategies, are all considered the means to a delightful end of ego-satisfaction. "All's fair in love and war," is stated as Christian and non-Christian women use people and scuttle their personal integrity. (Would you believe, for instance, that even Christian women will use their husbands and families to play games with other men?) It's a man trap, of course, but then, as one man (a Christian, yet!) told me, "she's lethal, but arsenic taken in small quantities is life-giving, you know." Pussycats are cute, and except for a few bad habits (which you mean to train of course) are fairly manageable. The trouble is, pussycats are tigers at heart. Man-eating tigers, that is. And when the pussycat grows up to be a tiger, the man is driven to the whip for sheer survival.

What happened to that adorable little game we used to play, you ask? You know, the one in which she played the puppet and I the big operator, I talked and she listened, she lavished me with flattery and I thought I was God. What happened is that two ego-trips headed toward each other are sure to collide, and rude will be the awakening, if not total calamity. What does a self-centered woman want? She wants you—for herself, and she will use any ruse to get what she wants. You call the pose; she will perform—but you will be the victim, and you will waken someday to the realization that you are the puppet and your manhood is dissipated to a hollow shell.

There is another kind of woman, rare and beautiful. Human? Yes, totally human, a whole person who, because she is totally committed to Jesus Christ and therefore God's woman, will not need to use you or anyone else to sustain her identity. She is free to be honest, loving, enjoying all of life to its fullest, and freeing you and all who meet her to enjoy life with her (or without her!). She is a woman of integrity, who will not compromise her spiritual wholeness by flaunting her sexuality or playing fraudulent games with anyone. She will not try to play God, nor will she expect you to play God with her. The dignity of her spiritual identity will be evident in her freedom to serve, but she will never serve your ego with flattery and deceit. She will speak the truth in love and gentleness, because she will want to make you God's man, not hers. She will satisfy your total manhood because in knowing her you are brought nearer to the God in whose image both you and she were made, and for whose glory you were intended to live. "She is a tree of life to those who lay hold of her; those who hold her fast are called happy." You will find that it is the indwelling Jesus Christ, her Lord, who makes her so, and you will want to praise him for his new creation! With such a woman, the Creator's plan of one woman joined to one man for lifelong union is not bondage but joyful freedom.

Why are such women so rare? Because, sir, you are demanding arsenic when you were designed by God to be sustained by living water. You too are human, subject either to God or Satan, ego-centered or God-centered in your perspective. Screened through your self-centeredness, the arsenic of sexual game-playing appears life-giving, and if you keep asking for it you will fill your life with toxin and the "every good thing" God intended for your humanity will turn to death, boredom, and futility. You will get what you expect from a woman: a plaything, a sop to your ego, or integrity of spirit, soul and body. Please, please, help us be what God intended: whole, mature, loving, sensitive, gentle, and gracious. You cannot make us so. Do not try to be God. Just give us godly, loving, sensitive leadership, so that we may see the Father in you and serve him in loving you and others.

I have never met a perfect person. I know some who are on the way to wholeness, and they make me and everyone who knows them love God. The God who filled them with himself and made them alive with beauty that is not contrived but genuine. They are growing people, honest people, struggling with truth and error, with reality and delusion—but in it all their sights are fixed on pleasing God first. He is teaching them how to love themselves and others as his people. They are learning that happiness is knowing God in the Lord Jesus Christ, who gives richness to every dimension of life.

A mature and whole woman wants you to be a mature and whole man—not for her ego-satisfaction, but for the sheer joy of knowing that you are becoming a total human being along with her. Counsel with her, she is your spiritual equal. Pray with her, give yourself to her as she gives herself to you, that you both may love and live to the glory of God, in the fullness of your humanity. If she is your wife, she is your first priority and commitment under God. If she is your sister-in-Christ, respect her as his woman. Women were not made for slavery, but God has asked us to follow your leadership. Please! Lead us not into temptation, but deliver us from game-playing and fraudulent living, that, as one people, we may exalt the name of Jesus Christ our Lord, and altogether be restored to the image and likeness of God as it is in his Son. Society must have the salt and light of honest, life-giving relationships in the people of God. You are responsible, under God, to give us that kind of leadership, and we are equally responsible under God to support you in that quality of headship.

May God give you the freedom to discuss and apply any truth you find in these pages with the women in your homes and churches, that we may together want what God wants. He is the giver of every good and perfect gift, the healer of our humanity. To him be glory in his temples, our bodies, and in his people, forever.